Mainstream Psychology

A Critique

Mainstream Psychology
A Critique

Braginsky and Braginsky
Wesleyan University   *Fairfield University*

HOLT, RINEHART AND WINSTON, INC.
New York Chicago San Francisco Atlanta
Dallas Montreal Toronto London Sydney

*Cover photograph of animal
experiment courtesy of
Pfizer, Inc.*

Abridgments, pp. 4, 13–14, in *The Manufacture of
Madness* by Thomas S. Szasz. Copyright © 1970 bv
Thomas S. Szasz. By permission of Harper & Row,
Publishers, Inc., and Routledge & Kegan Paul, Ltd.

Library of Congress Cataloging in Publication Data

Braginsky, Benjamin M.
  Mainstream psychology.

  Bibliography: p. 189
  1. Psychology: I. Braginsky, Dorothea D., joint
author II. Title. [DNLM: 1. Psychology.
BF121 B813m 1974]
BF38.B64   150   74-2157
ISBN: 0-03-085003-7
ISBN: 0-03-089514-6 (pbk.)

To the memory of Jules D. Holzberg

*A persistent but gentle scholar
deeply committed to the human condition
who illuminated the way for others.*

Foreword

In this book, the Doctors Braginsky have extended the lessons so well taught in their earlier books: that implicit extra-scientific commitments guide much of the activity of the practitioners of the normal science of psychology, that research and practice in psychology are directed by implicit principles and premises that have their origins in politics, in morality, and in bureaucracy.

Few will quarrel with the contention that the present unsatisfactory status of psychology is in great measure attributable to the inappropriate adoption of nineteenth-century physics as a model. In trying to emulate the objectivity of the prestigious natural sciences, psychologists conceived of human beings (and other organisms) as objects. Such a tour de force could only be accomplished as the result of intensive ideological preparation. The mechanistic metaphysic of mind, the belief in billiard ball causality, the artificial separation of morality from instrumentality, the ostrich-like posture that politics and religion are located in universes that do not intersect with science—these and other silent ideological strictures made possible the belief that men and women could be examined, inspected, manipulated, and dissected as if they were *things*. The findings wrought by the psychology that begins from the reification of persons has made little headway in influencing social policy. Rather, such a psychology, as the authors point out, is usually in the service of the power structure.

To recognize that psychology has an ideological base is, I believe, the first step toward saving us from total engulfment in oceans of trivia. More important, if future generations of psychologists can come to terms with the sometimes uncongenial fact that there is no end to ideology and that all decisions are made against a backcloth of implicit or explicit moral premises, then their efforts toward improving the common weal might come to fruition.

The authors of this penetrating book endeavor to remind us to examine our hidden assumptions. They take a hard look at currently active models of psychological science. The reader may at times despair that recovery from ideological infirmities is no longer possible, but the Braginskys do offer some keen suggestions for the restoration of health to psychology.

An anonymous student, considering the proposition that modern psychology be characterized as a Kuhnian paradigm-in-crisis, declared: "If there is a crisis, it is not because of a clash of competing paradigms. Rather it is the result of a belated *discovery* of ideology . . . such a discovery makes suspect nearly the whole enterprise of psychology." The pages that follow give ample voice to this insightful assertion.

Theodore R. Sarbin

Adlai E. Stevenson College
University of California, Santa Cruz

Preface

Mainstream psychology as a scientific enterprise is woven entirely from the political, economic, and moral threads of mainstream society. Psychologists, like the fabled Emperor and his new clothes, seem to enjoy the status and power that enables their nudity to go unnoticed. Yet, in recent years, it has become increasingly difficult for psychologists not to feel the chill of the real world. Many psychologists have responded by carefully and critically examining their own theories, research, and practices.

This manuscript represents just such an analysis of the mainstream movements of contemporary American psychology. Thus, this book is an extension of our earlier critiques of clinical psychology and psychiatry (Braginsky, Braginsky, & Ring, 1969; Braginsky & Braginsky, 1971). In these works, we found that clinical theories and practices were outgrowths of the values, beliefs, and moralities of society rather than of scientific facts. From the rarefied perspective of academic psychology, it might appear that these "practitioners" (who have been scientifically suspect) generated and maintained their clinical mythology by selectively avoiding the observations made by their laboratory-oriented colleagues.

Our analysis, however, suggested the opposite. The clinical myths and failures were, to a great extent, a function of the degree to which clinicians borrowed from and emulated mainstream academic psychology. In the present book, we take our analysis further by demonstrating that the myths and failures of academic psychology are a function of the degree to which it has borrowed from and emulated mainstream society. We have not conducted this analysis merely to indict psychology but to examine what is wrong in order to construct a more meaningful enterprise. Thus, this manuscript is replete with questions concerning where psychology has been, where it is at present, and where it might be going.

It is the intent of this book and our hope that the questions we, as well as others, have raised will lead to still more questions, which will ultimately define a psychology devoid of extraneous social, moral, and political influences. Therefore, this is not a professional or scientific etiquette manual, providing answers or rules of conduct for ritualized settings. To the contrary, our analysis explicates just how much of our professional thinking and behavior in the field of psychology is guided by social mores and taboos. The nature of this book makes it inconsistent, illogical, and inappropriate to provide new rules of conduct, which would have to be, at this time, based upon premature answers.

We are indebted to our friends, students, and colleagues who helped in the preparation of this manuscript. In particular, we thank our colleagues Doris Heyman, Vito Modigliani, Michael Kubovy, and Alexander Tolor for their valuable comments and suggestions. We also want to express our appreciation to Ohna Langer, Theresa Delco, and Jean Alberino, not only for their typing but for their intelligent involvement in preparing the manuscript.

An especially warm thank-you to Marilyn Braginsky, the family poet, who has tried to teach us how to write. Finally, we are indebted to Claudia and Craig for their significant reduction in noise and increase in sweetness and patience while we toiled at home.

The omission of the authors' initials does not mean that either one of us wants to avoid primary responsibility for this book or that we have dropped our first names. Instead, this is a desperate attempt to convince readers that our work is a truly collaborative effort, having no senior or junior author. The order in which the university affiliations appear on the title page offers no clue, since it is solely the expression of the editor's desire that they do not appear in a circle. For the reader's information, however, Dorothea D. Braginsky is in the Institute for Human Development at Fairfield University and Benjamin M. Braginsky is in the Psychology Department at Wesleyan University.

B. and B.

New Haven, Connecticut
February 1974

Contents

Foreword   vii

Preface   ix

1 **Psychology Today**   1

    What Do Psychologists Do?   5
    Scientist as "Moralizer"   5
    Scientist as "Mediator"   7
    Scientist as "Technician"   7
    Scientist as "Purist"   8
    Psychologist as Scientist   9
    The Scientific Enterprise   11
    Empirical Observation   12
    Operational Definition   13
    Statistical Generalization   14
    Prediction and Control   15
    The Design of Research   17

2 **The Sociology of Psychology**   25

    The Other History of Psychology   27
    Psychology and Religion   28
    Psychology and Politics   30
    Psychology and Every Day   36
    Searching the Soul of Psychology   39

3 **Method and Theory—The Heart of Behaviorism**   43

    The Behaviorist Movement   44
    The Methodolatry of Behaviorism   46

                                                      xiii

Behaviorist Jargon   58
Methodolatry and Jargon   62
The Skinnerian Approach   63
The Laws of Reinforcement and Extinction   66
Zog, Zoger, Zogment: The Paradigm   69

4 Technology and Others—The Heart of
   Humanistic Psychology   75

   Humanistic Jargon   77
   Humanistic Technolatry   83

5 Believing Is Seeing or Not Looking—
   I: Psychological Research   89

   The Rack as a Paradigm for Psychology   91
   Risks of the Rack   93
   Believing Is Not Looking   98
   Whom and What Psychologists Study   106

6 Believing Is Seeing or Not Looking—
   II: Psychological Diagnosis   111

   Who Are the Misfits?   114
   Psychodiagnosing the "Misfits"   117
   The Diagnosis of "Diagnosis"   120
   The Diagnosis of Diagnostic Labels   126
   Diagnoses as Stereotypes   129
   Labeling and Cleaning House   132

7 Psychotherapy   133

   Psychology's Psychotherapies   137
   What Is Psychotherapy?   139
   Might Makes Right: Behavior Modification   140
   Therapist as Food Pellet Dispenser   141
   Therapist as Pay Boss   144
   Therapist as One-Up-Man   146
   Therapist as Punisher   147
   Therapist as Emetic   150
   The Chamber of Horrors   151

Humanistic Psychotherapy   159
Other Voices, Other Rooms   162

8 Psychology Tomorrow   165

The Other Psychology   171
The Other Psychology of "Learning"   177
Psychology Now   186

References   189

Index   199

The psychologist finds himself in the midst of a rich and vast land full of strange happenings: There are men killing themselves; a child playing; a child forming his lips trying to say his first word; a person who, having fallen in love and being caught in an unhappy situation, is not willing or not able to find a way out; there is the mystical state called hypnosis, where the will of one person seems to govern another person; there is the reaching out for higher and more difficult goals; loyalty to a group; dreaming; planning, exploring the world; and so on without end. It is an immense continent full of fascination and power and full of stretches of land where no one has ever set foot.

Psychology is out to conquer this continent, to find out where its treasures are hidden, to investigate its danger spots, to master its vast forces, and to utilize its energies.

—Kurt Lewin, 1940

ONE

Psychology Today

As psychology approaches its centennial, its continued existence is under attack as never before in its history. In the past decade, the critics of psychology have grown more vocal, more passionate, more diverse, and more numerous. The criticisms range from the subtle, unspoken bewilderment of the introductory psychology student when he learns what psychology is *really* about, to the disaffection expressed by psychology graduate students, to the plea by a small number of professionals for changes, to the rebukes of allied professionals in law and medicine, to the vociferous criticisms of vice-presidents.

We are not dealing here with controversies or debates that threaten a theoretical posture or a particular methodology. Surely psychology is not new to controversy of this sort. The history of psychology is a sequence of one controversy following on the heels of (if not occurring simultaneously with) another. These have been documented as the "systems" or "schools" of psychology in an attempt to show just how far psychology has come. Instead, we are concerned with the criticisms that point out symptoms of an underlying malaise; symptoms that cannot

1

be debated away but must be remedied. If this is not done, psychology will suffer dearly. Many psychologists, aware of the increasing restrictiveness, narrowness, and irrelevancy of much of the vapid scholasticism in contemporary psychology, have expressed concern. Giorgi (1970) has catalogued the most frequently repeated themes critical of traditional psychology since the 1950s:

1. Psychology lacks real unity. (See Sonneman, 1954; MacLeod, 1965; Sanford, 1965; Koch, 1969)
2. Psychology lacks direction. (See Koch, 1959, 1969; Wolfle, 1959; Sanford, 1965)
3. Psychology should cease its strict emulaton of the natural sciences. (See Bugental, 1963; Sanford, 1965; Koch, 1959; Bakan, 1965, 1967, 1972)
4. Psychology has not been investigating meaningful phenomena in a meaningful way. (See Allport, 1955; Koch, 1969; MacLeod, 1965; Barker, 1968; Jordan, 1968)
5. Psychology lacks holistic methods. (See Sanford, 1965; MacLeod, 1965; Allport, 1955)
6. Traditional psychology does not do justice to the human person. (See Allport, 1955; Koch, 1961, 1969; Pervin, 1960; Sanford, 1965; Bakan, 1967)
7. Psychology's relevance to the life-world (Lebenswelt) is deficient. (See Sanford, 1965; Jordan, 1968; Barker, 1968; Koch, 1969)

After thirty years of intensive scholarly exploration concerning the possibilities of psychology becoming a significant enterprise, Sigmund Koch (1969) reluctantly concluded that "Whether as a 'science' or any kind of coherent discipline devoted to the empirical study of man, psychology has been misconceived." According to Koch, psychology has spent its one hundred years and its billions of man-hours in massing pseudoknowledge as a result of "ameaningful thinking." Jordan (1968) delivers a similar, though more histrionic, indictment of contemporary psychology:

There can be no doubt about it, contemporary American scientific psychology is the sterilest of the sterile. Years of arduous labor and the assiduous enterprise of hundreds of professors and thousands of students have yielded precisely nothing . . . Can one positive contribution towards an increased knowledge of man be pointed to? None such can be found; no substantive contribution can be named. The canard that "psychology is a new science" has long out-lived its explanatory-away usefulness; the unpleasant and discouraging facts must be faced honestly. (p. 230)

Krech (1969), in a volume memorializing William James (MacLeod, 1969), evaluated present day psychology a bit more generously:

As of *today*, the specific problems set for us by James 75 years ago, *as far as any solid work is concerned*, are pretty much where he left them. . . . Oh, we have gone some beyond James; we have found out a solid fact or two here, and even three or four quasi-solid facts there. . . . (p. 10)

Although Krech acknowledges some advances, his appraisal of psychology as a whole is rather a depressing one. In addition, many psychologists, upon reading the literature of mainstream American psychology, share the feelings articulated by Yospe (1972):

. . . I am frequently overcome by a profound sense of loss. It is an unwelcome feeling, singularly unpleasant, not entirely unlike the bereavement one suffers at the death of a loved one. . . . For the plain truth of the matter is that psychology, through some perverse cunning, has become alienated from itself . . . in reading today's psychological literature, one becomes increasingly aware that in many essential particulars psychology has lost contact with the very stuff, the very essence and spirit of that which originally gave it birth and implicit definition. In short, psychology has lost its moorings and has become separated from man. (pp. 2–3)

We, too, have experienced this sense of loss. This was, therefore, a difficult book for us to write, just as it will, at times, be painful for the readers who have also made a commitment to psychology. Moreover, to catalogue further the criticisms of contemporary psychology would be both boring and redundant. It is not our intention to recapitulate the critiques already presented so well by Koch (1959, 1969), Chein (1972), and other scholars. Suffice it to say that the state of affairs in psychology is appreciated by even the most casual participant in the psychological enterprise.

As psychologists, we are committed to the survival of psychology as a viable system for truth-seeking. Our analysis and criticisms, then, are borne out of concern that psychology is failing and has become alienated from itself. So long as its foundations are myths, absurdities, and pretensions, its demise is inevitable. Our purpose for writing this book, therefore, was that it may be used constructively in reshaping psychology.

Before we can proceed with this analysis, however, we must first define psychology; this is no easy task. Almost every student being introduced to psychology is told that *psychology is the scientific study of animal and human behavior* (or some similar variant). Not only do most students accept this definition without question, but so do most psychologists. And yet a moment's thought is enough to demonstrate that this definition is not only wrong but misleading as well. Psychology as a substantial whole does not exist. Moreover, it is questionable whether psychology could ever attain this status. Koch (1969) thinks that it is "finally clear that *psychology cannot be a coherent science,* or indeed a coherent field of scholarship. . . It can certainly not expect to become *theoretically* coherent . . . As for the *subject matter* of psychology, it is difficult to see how it could ever have been thought to be coherent. . ." In a similar vein, MacLeod (1965) remarks that psychology is a "crazy patchwork of all sorts of things, with a semblance of unity provided only by a common name and a place in the academic budget." In his attempt to define psychology, MacLeod (1965) was forced to ask: "Is psychology a subject, or a profession, or a profession disguised as a subject, or just a name in search of a meaning?"

Since we cannot turn to a body of knowledge, to a theoretical perspective, or even to a subject matter, we have no choice but to begin our exploration of psychology by examining the activities in which persons who are considered professional psychologists participate and the context of these activities. In part, then, we might begin our search by defining psychology in terms of what psychologists do.

What Do Psychologists Do?

The standard definition of psychology would lead us to believe that psychologists spend a good deal of their time scientifically observing animal and human behavior. The majority of the activities psychologists engage in, however, do not fall within the realm of this definition. Psychologists may lecture, grade papers, attend conferences, write research reports, participate in committees, seek promotions, conduct psychotherapy, or act as consultants. That is, they are engaged in activities that maintain (and usually increase) their economic and social status.

The division between ideal goals and reality is in no way peculiar to psychology but rather parallels the gap found in almost the entire scientific community. Blissett (1972) pointed out that although scientists are pledged to the impersonal search for truth, in reality, many aim only to better their own careers. At best, then, a small proportion of psychologists spend a small proportion of their time scientifically studying behavior even though the professional and, often, the personal identity of psychologists hinges on this very activity.

For the moment, then, in order to simplify our task, we will examine just the role of psychologist as scientist. Here, too, we find that "scientist" is a multidimensional, complex term used to describe many diverse postures and activities. Some of the roles scientists, particularly social scientists, play have been articulated by Sjoberg and Nett (1968): namely, scientist as "moralizer," "mediator," "technician," and "purist." The manifestations of these roles in the social sciences will be explored first, followed by a look at psychology in particular.

Scientist as "Moralizer"

Perhaps because social science has its roots in philosophy and religion, the first role taken by the social scientist was that of a "moralizer," insisting that the roots of the science be embedded in a moral framework. Thus, Comte viewed sociology as a "secular religion" dedicated to exorcising social evils. Later C. W. Mills called for the inextricable interweaving of scientific methods with ideological stances toward the crucial issues of the times. Most recently, Skinner (1971) has proposed that the knowledge he has acquired and the methods he has developed be used to change the basic "nature" of man if the world is to be saved. Most social scientists, unaware of the moral framework of their enterprise, propose and support value judgments that are accepted as "scientific knowledge."

Why do social scientists moralize, often unwittingly, under the guise of scientific neutrality? As we noted earlier, the social scientist is human, a person with many other pressures, many of which may penetrate the ambiguous, fluid boundaries of his professional life (e.g., popularity with students, obtaining grants, getting reports published, etc.). It is the very *texture* of the scientist's life that, according to Gouldner (1970), contradicts the autonomy of the scientific enterprise, and Sjoberg and Nett (1968) specify some of these textural components that lead to the role of moralizer:

> . . . the scientist seems to function most effectively as citizen-moralizer when he is enfolded in the cloak of scientific enterprise and its concomitant prestige and status. When the scientist speaks as an expert, the layman listens. What is more, *power* and *authority* tend to accrue to the scientist who moralizes, who seeks to shape men's actions (the ultimate goal of moralization) . . . In the end, the fundamental dilemma facing the scientist is the need to moralize in order to sustain and to *legitimize* the *scientific method* and its use in the search for objective truth . . . So the very process of *self-justification* can structure one's scientific findings. Similarly, the researcher wishing to give a good account of himself may limit his studies to those that *conform* to, or at least do not clash with, the *moral stance* of the group or society he is researching. But this too may detract from the validity of his findings. (pp. 88–89; italics ours)

Thus, we see not only some of the reasons for assuming this role, but also some of the scientific difficulties the role of moralizer may present.

Scientist as "Mediator"

The transformation of the scientist's role into "mediator" of knowledge not only retains the pitfalls of moralizing, but adds some new ones as well. Specifically, the mediator is just as enmeshed in the moral framework of his profession and society as the explicit moralizer, but the mediator publicly announces a *neutral* position. He presents his task as mediating between conflicting theories and ideologies, policy decisions, research findings. As a peace-keeper attempting to resolve these conflicts, he maintains that the "truth" exists somewhere between the competing positions.

Neutrality, however, may not be an effective source of truth and knowledge. The history of science abounds with illustrations of progress resulting from the head-on clash between competing ideologies and theories. Peace-keeping by seeking compromise or neutral ground may resolve the conflict while destroying the possibility of discovery. Thus, stressing pragmatism and eschewing ideological commitment may often be antithetical to the search for knowledge.

Scientist as "Technician"

To become a "technician" is a simple transformation; the only requirement is that the scientist make himself available to business, government, or other institutional enterprise. The allegiance of the scientist is to the organization; his primary and, perhaps, sole obligation is to solve the problems that confront the organization. His work is concrete; there is little room for speculating or theorizing. He must solve the particular problem by using the scientific skills of research design, statistics, polling techniques, and so on. The morality, ethics, or politics of the scientist should not intervene in the solution of the problem.

The role of the technician-scientist, in fact, appears to necessitate the suspension of moralization in order to deal effectively and efficiently with the specific organization's tasks. Indeed, the apparent suspension of morality has led to public outcry upon learning that some scientists work as diligent technicians inventing new products, as well as better techniques to sell them, that are hazardous to the health of the consumer, or devising methods to exterminate masses of people, such as biological and thermonuclear weapons.

However, this explanation of the amoral behavior of scientist-technicians is erroneous. The technician is also committed to a moral stance. The difference between the moralizer and the technician is that the technician accepts implicitly the morality of his organization while the moralizer attempts to define his position on the basis of his own personal morality.

Scientist as "Purist"

The ideal role of the scientist, which is passed on to students of science, is that of the "purist." Here, the researcher, divorced from extrascientific concerns, engages in *pure* research: research that does not have to be justified to the general public. It is conducted simply for the pleasure of discovery, adding new knowledge to the subject matter of science.

Greenberg (1967) describes scientists' reverence for pure or basic research as tinged with evangelism, chauvinism, and xenophobia. Many researchers, he notes, proudly compare the scientific enterprise with the construction of the great cathedrals of the Middle Ages and the pyramids of the ancient Egyptians. Unfortunately, the scientist as purist is also primarily a moralist, although his morality is shared only by his colleagues. The scientist argues that pure research must be supported (usually by public funds) as a monument to contemporary civilization, neglecting to see the monstrous tolls such monuments have exacted in the past from the masses who were to be elevated by these edifices. Greenberg (1967) points out that, at least in the past, the masses could see and appreciate the monuments that were constructed; the scientific monument, on the other hand, is visible mainly to its creators—the scientists.

The rationale offered by the advocates of pure science, be they social, biological, or physical scientists, is that without basic research, the technology of today would have been impossible to achieve. The straight line from science to technology, from knowledge to utility posited by the purists, does not bear up under closer scrutiny. On the basis of his investigation of the relationship between science and technology, Greenberg (1967) concluded that: "there has prevailed an interaction of such incredibly complex and intricate composition that it is rarely possible in examining artifact or device to sift the science from the technology." A cursory historical investigation shows that Watt's steam engine was invented before knowledge of the Carnot cycle; that navigators recognized magnetism as an empirical fact centuries before physicists studied the phenomenon; the techniques of lens grinding preceded the development of the microscope and telescope; and so on.

In 1963, the Department of Defense undertook Project Hindsight, a study to determine the relationship between twenty weapons in the U.S. arsenal and the billions of dollars spent supporting pure research over a period of twenty years. The findings of this project disclosed that a mere two events (4/10 of 1 percent) of the more than 500 events leading to the development of the weapons fell under the definition of pure science, 8 percent under applied science, and the remaining 92 percent under technology (see Greenberg, 1967). Thus, when dealing with concrete criteria, even the purists in the hard sciences are left with no rationale for pure research other than monument-building.

Psychologist as Scientist

As a scientist, the psychologist may adopt any one of the stances previously described, but the two most popular seem to be the "moralizer" and the "purist." In the role of moralizer it becomes clear why some psychologists in the Soviet Union scientifically conclude that persons who express deviant political attitudes are schizophrenic; why a prominent American psychologist labels radical college students as paranoid; why Barry Goldwater was diagnosed (without ever having met him) by over 1000 psychiatrists for *Fact Magazine* as "unfit psychologically" to be president; why research psychologists demonstrate that "democratic" groups are better than "authoritarian" ones, and that blacks are intellectually inferior to whites. It is merely human that a psychologist chooses to support the political system (and its ancillary values) in his professional work if it means his professional and, perhaps, personal destruction should he fail to support that system.

There is another inescapable reason why psychologists act as moralizers: the very heart of psychology, even that which lives in the animal laboratory, is a moral system. Thus, as soon as one accepts the role of psychologist, he is transformed into a scientist-moralizer, adopting an extrascientific posture imposed by cultural values. Indeed, MacLeod (1965) has noted that psychology is so culture bound that it fails to shed light on that which it should be studying. To be sure, the cultural values, mores, and taboos that psychologists accept are couched in scientific jargon, appearing both objective and neutral. Yet, these values function in the same way political and religious values function within their systems: namely, to control the types of observations one makes, the interpretations of these observations, and the "truths" and "facts" that are acceptable. Later, we will return to this point and explore in depth the morality that underlies psychological theories and methods as well as its outcomes.

As "purists" psychologists may, perhaps, participate in fruitless scientific activity. In addition, the present accumulation of data awaits compilation into a coherent body of knowledge. The purists recognize their own limitations with regard to this enormous and, according to Koch (1969), impossible task. Yet the favorite delusion of the purist psychologist, described by MacLeod (1965), is "that of the man in a white coat, in a roomful of glittering gadgets, one hand adjusting a microscope and the other poised over a calculating machine. We love it, and our students love it. If only we could project this image on television, our happiness would be complete."

Other roles for the scientist could no doubt be added to this list (such as scientist as "guru" or as "window-dressing"). The point we wish to make is that the term "scientist" cannot be used in a simple, unidimensional way without obscuring what science is and what scientists do. At best, then, the word "scientist" tells us that there are some people in our society who are labeled differently from others; at worst, the word conjures up images of mythical men performing mythical functions.

Clearly, some of the strategies presented above may have greater potential than others in facilitating knowledge. But with all these diverse roles available to scientists, how do the institutions of science function to advance knowledge? The institutionalization of science is itself an attempt to insure its own advancement (e.g., requirements of arduous graduate training in the uses of specialized techniques, scientific method, etc.). In addition, the difficulty scientists have had in weeding out the erroneous, in honoring the worthy, and in advancing the truth has led to the evolution of a complex system of certification to provide some checks and balances. Greenberg (1967) has likened this intricate system to the western process of jurisprudence, noting that science is probably as often in error (hanging the innocent while acquitting the guilty) but "enjoys the luxury of reversing its error."

The lesson to be learned from the history of science is that the *scientific method* does not necessarily lead to reliable and valid theories, methods, or information. Even if a scientist is accurately following the scientific method, it does not necessarily follow that he is correct in his assumptions, techniques, or findings. What then differentiates the scientific enterprise from other human enterprises?

The Scientific Enterprise

To even begin to explore the question of "what is science?", as Ziman (1968) points out:

> . . . is almost as presumptuous as to try to state the meaning of Life itself. This question has long been debated. Famous books have been devoted to it. It has been the theme of whole schools of philosophy. To give an account of all the answers with all the variations, would require a history of western thought. It is a daunting subject. (pp. 1–2)

It would be inappropriate (and no doubt impossible) to answer this question here. Instead, let us examine some of the more commonly agreed upon rules governing scientific inquiry; those rules and regulations that are assumed to differentiate science from magic, philosophy, pseudoscience, and common sense. The rules selected for scrutiny are those that are especially characteristic of scientific psychology: (1) the principle of empirical observation; (2) the principle of operational definition; (3) the principle of statistical generalization; (4) the principle of prediction and control.

Empirical Observation

A descriptive statement is regarded as true if and only if it is found to correspond with observed reality. The ultimate test of the truth or falsity of an empirical statement is the *test of observation* . . . "Observed reality" is not easily defined, but it will be adequate for our purpose to define it as sense data (which rules out intuition and divine revelation) on which different observers agree (which rules out hallucinations). (Anderson, 1971, pp. 24–25)

The principle of empirical verification, according to Anderson (1971) as well as most every scientist, is the single most important principle for scientific description to which the three other principles are subordinated. Yet, when we eliminate the jargon in Anderson's statement, such as "sense data" and "test of observation," it reads very simply: *seeing is believing*. If this is *the* principle for all science, then all men are scientists. People are continuously engaged in making observations in order to test either their own or others' beliefs. Yet, scientists seem to have made this principle exclusively their own. Furthermore, we also know that seeing is not always believing, and that often what we believe makes us *see*. At one time, great scholars and scientists "saw" a flat world, a solar system that revolved around the earth, and the works of witches and devils. However, scientists, like other people, can be wrong in their observations of the external world; plurality is not a sufficient criterion for determining the truth or falsity of a proposition. Thus, "empirical observation" has no built-in safeguards to protect us from illusions, hallucinations, intuition, divine revelation, or our own blindness.

Operational Definition

All terms in a descriptive statement must be carefully defined in terms of the operations involved in manipulating or observing their referents . . . The principle of operational definition requires us to "point to" the things we are talking about. Such statements, to which the test of observation can be applied, are called testable statements. Only such statements are scientific. (Anderson, 1971, pp. 26–27)

Even a cursory look at this principle leads us to conclude that all people, not just scientists, have been doing this for a very long time. The hostess serving dinner does not rely solely on her guests' verbal approval of her cooking, but instead weighs more heavily the quantity of the food consumed, the gusto with which it was eaten, and so on. The man buying a new car does not rely solely upon the salesman's verbal description, but insists upon a test drive.

Again, if the specific vocabulary such as "operational," or "referents," is simplified, we recognize this activity in other areas. The testing of the religious commitment of Abraham and of Job shows just how ageless and universal this principle is. But does it work? Is this at least a foolproof guide to truth and knowledge? Obviously not. A look at some of the applications of this principle demonstrates the possibility for error.

At one time, guilt and innocence were operationally defined by taking a suspect, tying his hands and feet to a large pole, and dunking him under water for varying periods of time. If he drowned, he was guilty. If he survived, he was innocent. The operations and the referents (either breathing or not breathing) can be "pointed to." Thus, guilt and innocence transformed into testable statements could be called scientific assertions. Operationalism standing alone, without the help of the other principles, obviously is not science. Clearly, there are a number of difficulties inherent in this principle, but, as Ziman (1968) points out, "Scientists do not in fact work the way operationalists suggest; they tend to look for, and find, in Nature little more than they believe to be there, and yet they construct airier theoretical systems than their actual observations warrant." We shall return to this point later in the book.

Statistical Generalization

You can generalize an observation to conditions other than those under which it was made if the conditions under which it was made constitute an adequate random sample from the set of conditions to which you wish to generalize. (Anderson, 1971, p. 25)

Of all the principles reviewed thus far, statistical generalization sounds the most scientific. Simply stated, however, much of the scientific aura is lost. People generalize from a small number of experiences to more encompassing areas, usually staying within the bounds of logic. Thus, a teacher who observes a child's outstanding performance in reading and math might conclude that the child is scholastically "bright." The teacher would not, however, comment upon the child's physical prowess or music ability. This seems to be based upon common sense, but common sense does not always lead to knowledge. For instance, stereotypy, a frequent form of generalization, suggests that on the basis of a few experiences with a few members of a group, generalizations about the entire group are made. For example, all Germans are seen as punctilious, all Mexicans as lazy, all college students as radicals, and so on. Although the principle of generalization represents man's attempt to order and understand his world, it often degenerates into stereotypy, distorting and obscuring that which he wants to understand.

The scientist, on the other hand, assumes that he is safeguarded from making erroneous generalizations, since he may randomize his sample, use statistical methods, and make probability statements concerning his observations. There is a growing number of psychologists, however, who recognize that statistical procedures do not assure "truth." Aware of the dangers of statistical generalization, they have introduced concepts such as concurrent validity, predictive validity, and ecological validity.

Despite sophisticated statistical procedures, they contend that logical errors may occur when generalizing from a small sample to a large universe, much less from animal studies to people.

Most psychologists engaged in research activity realize that statistical procedures do not guarantee objectivity or meaningful results. These statistical procedures are the tools of the craft, and like all tools, they are only as good as the craftsman who uses them. The most striking illustration of this, though embarrassing to the social scientists who conducted the poll, was the prediction of the outcome of the presidential contest between Roosevelt and Landon. After employing an apparently ideal randomization procedure (picking names at random from telephone directories) as well as sophisticated statistical procedures, all of the results indicated that Landon would win by a landslide victory. The researchers, however, did not take into consideration the millions of working-class voters who had no telephones, citizens who largely voted for Roosevelt.

The most illogical experiment or the most spuriously related phenomenon can yield a statistic. In short, statistical generalization does not provide wisdom or foolishness; both are a function of the intelligence and good sense of the investigator who uses these procedures.

Prediction and Control

Prediction and control, stated earlier as a principle, has become for most psychologists the goal of the scientific enterprise. Indeed, many psychologists might argue that our presentation of the principles of empirical observation, operational definition, and statistical generalization out of the context of prediction and control was a misrepresentation. When the three principles are viewed in the service of prediction and control, then you have science. However, the primary importance attributed to control and prediction, upon close inspection, cannot be upheld. As Ziman (1968) indicates:

It arbitrarily excludes pure mathematics, and needs to be supplemented to take cognizance of those perfectly respectable sciences such as Astronomy or Geology where we can only observe the consequence of events and circumstances over which we have no control. It also fails to give due credit to the strong theoretical and logical sinews that are needed to hold the results of experiments and observations together and give them force. (p. 4)

The emphasis on prediction and control not only by fiat excludes some of man's greatest achievements (e.g., zoology, philology, oceanography, and, in fact, the theory of evolution); as a principle of science, it is not appropriate. One can accurately predict and effectively control behavior on the basis of myths as well as understanding and knowledge. For instance, one can predict a person's susceptibility to hypnosis and control the hypnotized person's behavior on the basis of a theory of animal magnetism.

The roots of psychology's almost exclusive commitment to prediction and control have been traced by Bakan (1967) to the "mystery-mastery" complex in contemporary psychology, a complex that has been a major source of interference with understanding and the acquisition of knowledge. The literature is full of methodological critiques ("self-fulfilling prophecy," "experimenter bias," "demand characteristic of the experiment," "the Hawthorne effect," and so on), which raises serious questions about what it is we are predicting and controlling, and what exactly are the bases of these predictions. It seems that extraexperimental variables often produce behaviors identical to that predicted on the basis of "scientific theories" both in animal and human subjects.

Nonetheless, prediction and control may be one of many principles used to bolster an argument, theory, or ideology. But, once again, we are dealing with a principle that is not the exclusive property of scientists. The man of religion, of politics, of business and industry, as well as the man-in-the-street, all have a vested interest in predicting and controlling interactions with other people.

Thus, on the basis of the discussion of these four principles of science, in addition to the recent controversies concerning scientific method (with advocates debating the advantages and disadvantages of abduction and retroduction, logico-deduction, hypothetico-deduction, induction, sensitizing conceptions, dialecticism, and logical relativism), it is clear that we do not know what it is that differentiates "scientific" inquiry from other forms of inquiry. Ziman (1968), after an intensive review of the definitions of science, concluded that:

> What one finds in practice is that scientific argument, written or spoken, is not very complex or logically precise . . . This is not said to disparage the intellectual powers of scientists; I mean simply that the reasoning used in scientific papers is not very different from what we should use in an everyday careful discussion of an everyday problem. (p. 8)

To refute the conclusion that scientists think, argue, and obtain data about the world in much the same way as most other people, one may wish to point to the signs of scientific accomplishment. Automobiles, miracle drugs, heart transplants, and spaceships to the moon are all examples of successful scientific problem-solving. On the other hand, one may also point to the development of language, survival on a battlefield or in a ghetto, and evolution of institutions, as instances of successful extrascientific problem solving. Because the problems differ, we are often led to assume that the thought processes involved in their solution also are different, but there is no evidence to substantiate this impression.

What then, if anything, distinguishes the problem-solving behaviors of scientists from those of the man-in-the-street? Obviously, the content, complexity and, sometimes, the importance of the problems vary. In addition, the scientist has greater control over the subject matter and the context in which it is studied than the layman. However, greater control, as we shall soon see, does not always enhance the accuracy of the solution of the problem under study. The steps involved in the design of psychological research will illustrate this.

The Design of Research

All research starts with a general question such as "Is X related to Y?", "Does X cause Y?", and so on. The scientist then makes an educated guess about the possible answer—that is, he formulates an hypothesis (eg., "X is related to Y"). Then a test is devised in order to verify or disprove the hypothesis. If the research is well thought out, and if a number of possible errors are not made, an answer will be forthcoming. There is no guarantee, however, that a spurious finding or a false conclusion will not occur. Nonetheless, the data are examined and the hypothesis is either confirmed, rejected, or held suspended pending further research. This is, of course, an oversimplification, but it represents the basic, explicit outline for laboratory studies.

This conception of research, then, consists only of testing hypotheses. Bakan (1967), in a critical vein, notes that: "Curiosity, interest in the phenomena, or even the complex psychodynamics associated with the getting of hypotheses are brushed aside . . . by the time the investigatory enterprise has reached the stage of testing hypotheses, most of the important work, if there has been any, has already been done." He likens psychologists to children playing cowboys, where they emulate everything but the cowboys' main work—taking care of cows. Similarly, psychologists somehow appear to "play scientist" and avoid the major work of scientists, which is making meaningful discoveries.

However misconstrued, testing hypotheses is not only the work of scientists but a daily activity engaged in by all people. A man in the process of crossing a busy intersection in Manhattan, for example, takes the following steps (although, admittedly, he may be unaware of the process): The general question here is, "Will I be able to cross this street safely?" The hypothesis he formulates might be, "Yes, I can cross this street." As he starts across the street, we can be sure that he guessed that he would be able to arrive at the other side safely, and that he is in the process of testing that hypothesis. Hopefully, he will be correct and will continue along his way.

One might propose that there is a crucial difference between the scientists' and the man-in-the-street's hypothesis testing that we have omitted: namely, that scientists are impersonal and objective; they are removed from the process of verification, while the man in the street is not. Moreover, no matter how strongly the scientist wants his hypothesis to be confirmed, this desire should not have an effect on the outcome of his experiment. The ordinary man, personally enmeshed in the situation, may distort the outcome by numerous defensive strategies. For example, a young man may receive an invitation to a party. He does not want to go, since he is convinced that the party will be dull and that he will have a miserable time. Several friends prevail upon him to attend the party and test his hypothesis. He goes reluctantly. Shortly after his arrival, he concludes that he had been correct; the party is indeed dull.

As observers of this situation, we would not conclude that this young man made a fair, unbiased, empirical test of his hypothesis. We recognize the strong possibility that the reluctant party-goer may have gone out of his way to have a boring time. That is, he engaged in a "self-fulfilling prophecy." He was able, therefore, to distort the outcome of his "experiment." Scientists, on the other hand, do not have this kind of control over the outcomes of their experiments. Or do they?

If we examine the domain of the psychologist engaged in research, we find that he has far greater control over the experimental situation than the man-in-the-street could possibly have over his domain, since he has the potential for creating and shaping almost every significant aspect of his empirical arena. Beginning with the question he asks, how he formulates his hypothesis, the kind of data he accepts to test his hypothesis, to the final conclusions he draws on the basis of his findings, the psychologist is in complete control. From beginning to end, the psychological experiment is a contrivance of the investigator.

The control of phenomena and the situations in which they occur is not necessarily a negative activity. This kind of control does imply, however, that there is a strong chance that personal and social forces will intrude in, and thereby bias, any or all aspects of the psychological experiment (see Orne, 1962; Rosenthal, 1966). As Harre (1970) states in his critical review of the experimental situation: "The laboratory is but another situation, and the experiment but another episode, within which the 'scientist' dwells, negotiating his own identity and providing his own excuses and justifications. All he gets back in response are the excuses and justifications of his subjects."

The psychologist's situational control may, in fact, render him more vulnerable to biases and, therefore, make his conclusions more incorrect than even our party-goer's. The young man at the party has far less control over the situation than the psychologist has over his laboratory. Thus, the party-goer may be pleasantly surprised, after meeting a very attractive young woman at the party, and happily admit that his earlier hypothesis had been wrong. The research psychologist, however, once having chosen a course, structures his laboratory world in accordance with this course, leaving little room for the possibility of a surprise outcome, which is usually the basis for discovery. Indeed, such surprises are rarely pleasant, since it means that something went wrong, structurally or conceptually, in the fabrication of the experimental situation.

In short, the psychological experimenter is at least as personally and deeply involved in the phenomena he wishes to understand, predict, and control as any other person. The commitment to formulate "correct" hypotheses (reinforced by the publication standards of professional journals and the promotion standards of universities) makes the psychologist perhaps more susceptible to influences that can distort his conclusions. The psychologist, thus, is faced with a choice: using the maximal. controls necessary to conduct his research, he can either find the "truth" or continue to perpetrate a myth.

Many psychologists are aware that without the "cosmetics" of science—the lab coats, white rats, IBM printouts, T mazes, intelligence tests, jargon, and assorted paraphernalia —it is hard to know exactly what makes them scientists. Indeed, Skinner (1953) in his attempt to define science and scientists, unwittingly has brought the psychologist back into the folds of humanity:

Science is first of all a set of attitudes. It is a disposition to deal with the facts rather than with what someone has said about them . . . Science is a willingness to accept facts even when they are opposed to wishes. Thoughtful men have perhaps always known that we are likely to see things as we want to see them instead of as they are, but thanks to Sigmund Freud we are today much more clearly aware of "wishful thinking." The opposite of wishful thinking is intellectual honesty—an extremely important possession of the successful scientist . . . the practice of science puts an exceptionally high premium on honesty . . . Scientists have also discovered the value of remaining without an answer until a satisfactory one can be found. This is a difficult lesson. It takes considerable training to avoid premature conclusions, to refrain from making statements on insufficient evidence and to avoid explanations which are pure invention . . . Science is, of course, more than a set of attitudes. It is a search for order, uniformities, for relations among the events in nature. (pp. 12–13)

Skinner's statement is an attempt at a moral code, describing how a scientist should act and the qualities he should possess, qualities and behaviors that have been told over and over to western man. The "commandments" of science are shared by millions of people who believe that a person should be open-minded and fair, honest, tolerant, and patient. We cannot conclude that these ideals set scientists apart from other fair-minded people.

Thus, when we sift through the intellectual cosmetics, the theories and principles of science, and the processes that comprise the scientific method, we find that there is no way to differentiate the scientific enterprise from other human enterprises. It would pose no threat to the biochemist or the physicist to learn that science is a human enterprise and that scientists are human. On the other hand, social scientists would be most defensive about this point, since the subject matter, the raw materials, and conclusions of their scientific endeavors are human as well.

To admit to the humanness of psychology is, in part, to recognize that much of what psychology is today—its theories, techniques, methodologies, and areas of inquiry—has been constructed and shaped by social forces, some of which are antithetical to the pursuit of knowledge and understanding. That a psychologist is human does not necessarily indicate that his science is wrong. It is this very humanness that may lead to creativity and diversity in the scientific enterprise. A number of psychologists (see Giorgi, 1970) have emphasized the need to be more human in their approach in order to remove psychology from the sterile wasteland it appears to inhabit. But, to be ignorant of being human, or, still worse, to ignore it believing that one's scientific objectivity will make it disappear is to be totally led astray. As Sjoberg and Nett (1968) have noted:

> . . . the scientist is influenced not only by his theoretical commitment but by his role and status in society. To treat the scientist as a non-person is to ignore social reality . . . For as long as researchers are human beings engaged in the study of their fellow man they must examine their own values and roles, both in science and in the society at large. (p. 71)

Scholars in nearly every field of endeavor (e.g., Kuhn, 1962; Myrdal, 1969; Polanyi, 1958) have begun to appreciate the role of man, his values, goals, and beliefs, as well as his creativity, in the acquisition of knowledge. Yet, as Yospe (1972) points out, "in the swirl of all this activity, psychology stands almost alone and untouched . . . [clinging] tenaciously to a philosophically defunct logical positivism and operationism." Koch (1964) too notes that psychology, "almost alone in the scholarly community . . . remains in the grip of the old conception [of knowledge]."

The failure of psychology to deal with man's place in human knowledge allows these forces (values, goals, beliefs) to function unnoticed, distorting and obfuscating the reality it purports to represent.

The recognition of the interplay among social, personal, and scientific forces should lead psychologists to thoughtful inquiry into the nature of this relationship. Instead, we find that most psychologists are undaunted, and rely heavily on the scientific method to negate human influences and enable them to perform their research free of the myths, fallacies, values, and needs of society at large. Bergmann and Spence (1944) went so far as to "methodologically" separate the psychologist from the subject matter by providing an "epistemological sophistication": " . . . the empiricist scientist should realize that his behavior, symbolic or otherwise, does not lie on the same methodological level as the responses of his subjects." Furthermore, Bergmann and Spence point out that ". . . the experiences of the observing scientist do indeed have a privileged, even unique, position."

Nothing that we have been able to note thus far justifies elevating the scientific empiricist to such a privileged position. The evidence that has been compiled in recent years (again, see Orne, 1962; Rosenthal, 1966), indeed, the entire history of science, amply documents the error of such deification. All types of psychological research are susceptible to the frailties of the experimenter despite the purity of his mind or his method.

The human endeavor to create or discover new knowledge is extremely vulnerable to error. The psychologist is perhaps more vulnerable than most other scientists, not only for the reasons enumerated above, but because the psychologist must face another major obstacle. Specifically, psychologists must maintain their professional territory. The physicist, the chemist, or the geologist is reasonably safe from the fear of outsiders usurping his terrain—a terrain that takes years of arduous labor and serious study to master. Everyone, however, seems to be familiar with psychology in one form or another. Salesmen, clergymen, physicians, dentists, con-men, butchers, housewives, teachers, even nursery school children use "psychology." Indeed, in order to function successfully in modern-day society, people must be able to understand, predict, and control their own, as well as other people's behavior. Thus, psychologists must strive to set apart their enterprise from the endeavors of the rest of the population, since the layman's attempt to understand, predict, and control his environment can come in conflict with the endeavors made by psychologists. In their attempt to retain and protect their profession from unqualified individuals, psychologists have glorified and developed, to an extreme, the cosmetics of science, replacing knowledge with jargon and technology with ritual. Surely this defensive posture can only be a hindrance to the scientific enterprise. The psychologist, as a result, spends too much of his time perfecting his role as a scientist at the expense of perfecting his science.

It is clear that within the field of psychology there exists the potential, and too many opportunities to realize the potential, for going astray. The direction in which mainstream American psychology has wandered, why it has wandered so far afield, and what other, more constructive paths it might follow will be explored in the remaining chapters.

TWO

The Sociology of Psychology

Although many of the sciences may be justly accused of lacking an historical approach to their subject (see Larrabee, 1966), psychology, at least, has attempted to embed its theories and methodologies in history. Almost every department of psychology offers a course to its advanced students in the History of Psychology. Indeed, every introductory textbook, as well as most advanced texts, provides in the first few pages an historical context for psychology.

Nearly all of these accounts begin with Aristotle, the "father" of almost everything modern, and generally include luminaries such as Descartes, Hobbes, Locke, Hume, and so on. The influences of the natural sciences upon psychology are often spelled out, too, paralleling psychological theories and methods with the theories and discoveries in the natural sciences. For example, the theories of Darwin, Helmholtz, Pearson, and the findings in physics, biology, and physiology are shown to have played a vital role in the intellectual development and direction of modern psychology.

The point of the discourse reads as follows: "Thus psychology grew out of philosophy, and its history is intermingled with the history of philosophy and of other sciences" (Hilgard, 1962). The history of psychology, then, is presented as a history of ideas, ignoring completely those nonintellectual areas of life which, as we shall see, had a far greater impact upon the creation, direction, and maintenance of psychology: namely, religion, politics, and economics. It seems to be a glaring oversight to present psychology closely wedded to philosophy and natural science while conceptually divorced from the rest of the world around it. That the compilers of psychology's history altogether neglected to relate the conceptions of man, of "human nature," and the conditions of man during the periods explored to the ongoing religious-political-economic conceptions calls out for some explanation. As Myrdal (1969) points out: "Ignorance, like knowledge, is purposefully directed."

In its quest for establishing itself as a respectable and credible scientific enterprise, psychology wisely proposed that its roots are in philosophy, the forebearer of mathematics and physics. Philosophy, a high-brow, high-minded discipline, is no doubt a more respectable influence than the rather mundane religious, political, and economic forces. The latter are just not good company for a science which, as we noted earlier, uses its history in an attempt to show how far it has come as a science.

The selective presentation, nonetheless, upon close inspection falls short of its objective. Koch's (1969) summary of the 100-year history of "scientific" psychology depicts a different series of events:

> . . . "scientific" psychology can now be seen to be a succession of changing doctrines about *what* to emulate in the natural sciences —especially physics. Each such strategic doctrine was entertained not as conditional upon its cognitive fruits but functioned rather as a security fetish bringing assurance to the psychologist, and hopefully the world, that he was a scientist. [The various experimental paradigms] succeeded each other not by virtue of differential productivity, but rather because of the dawning recognition that significant problems and segments of subject

matter were being evaded—or because of boredom with the old paradigm. (pp. 64, 66)

The point remains that the religious, political, and economic domains have been excluded from the historical accounts of psychology's evolution. Indeed, it may be feared that the recognition of the relationship between psychology and these domains might vitiate, and perhaps even endanger, the psychological enterprise. The remainder of this chapter, as well as a large portion of the rest of the book, will explore the nature of this relationship and its effects upon the functional roles of psychologists.

The Other History of Psychology

The religious, political, and economic influences on the social sciences have been examined by Merton (1967), Myrdal 1969), and Gouldner (1970), among others. Although none of these men are psychologists, their analyses, nonetheless, apply equally to psychology as to their own disciplines.

Merton (1967), in his essay, "Puritanism, Pietism and Science," details the impact of the religious ethos of seventeenth-century England on science. He concludes that although the religious reformers were not enthusiastic about science, "the religious ethic which stemmed from Calvin promoted a state of mind and a value-orientation which invited the pursuit of natural science." Surely, one might suggest, this is ancient history bearing little resemblance to either the state of mind or the ethos of scientists today. But as Merton (1967) remarks:

. . . once a value-orientation of this kind becomes established, it develops some degree of functional autonomy, so that the predilection for science could remain long after it has cut away from its original theological moorings . . . this pattern of orientation, which can even now be detected statistically, may be unwitting and below the threshold of awareness of many of those involved . . . the highly visible interaction of the institutions of science and religion—as in the so-called war between the two in the Nineteenth Century—may obscure the less visible, indirect and perhaps more significant relationship between the two. (p. 606)

Psychology and Religion

The close relationship between religion and science need not dismay the scientist or the student of science since, as Bakan (1967) notes, "both religion and science are attempts on the part of mankind to search out the nature of himself and the world in which he lives." Indeed, both religion and science represent what Myrdal (1969) calls those "higher valuations" of man, which are usually relegated to the shadows of everyday life and taken out only for ceremonial occasions. Ideally, then, the scientist by obeying the commandments of science (honesty, openness, patience, tolerance, and fairmindedness) represents the very best in the Judeo-Christian tradition.

Unfortunately, just as some men of the cloth shadow their "higher valuations" with more mundane, opportunistic ones, so do some scientists; just as some men of the cloth are tempted by idolatry, and at times succumb, so do some scientists. Bakan (1967) parallels the danger present for both when he states that "as soon as either the scientist or the theologian allows himself to be *fixed upon an answer as though it were the ultimate fulfillment of his impulse,* then indeed does he stop being either scientist or theologian and becomes an *idolater"* (italics ours).

The social scientist armed with his empirical observations, operational definitions, statistical generalizations, and a preoccupation with prediction and control is a far better candidate for idolatry than the man of religion. The religious man is made aware by his training of the danger of idolatry and is held in check by the "sinfulness" of it. No such awareness or check is available to the social scientist. Instead, he is led to believe that his training makes him immune to such dangers. Yet, as Bakan (1967) describes it, the very essence of idolatry is already present in the social sciences, especially psychology: "Idolatry is the *loss of the sense of search,* of the sense of freshness of experience. It is the overquick *fixing upon any method or device or concept* . . . Idolatry is the *impulse to be bribed* by incomplete but immediate satisfaction" (italics ours).

In the scientific enterprise idolatry may be transformed into "methodolatry," the worship of methods, "quantophenia," "testomania," and "the bribe," publication of results leading to promotions, prestige, and so on. In this light, then, the favorite image of experimental psychologists disclosed by MacLeod (1965), "the man in a white coat, in a roomful of glittering gadgets . . ." loses its intended humor. The clinical psychologist, the school psychologist, and the industrial personnel psychologist, with their reliance upon a battery of tests to answer their questions concerning the "inner nature" of their subject, have all given up the search for the security of "answers." They are convinced by statistical norms and charts that these tests are the instruments of intrapsychic detective work.

A cursory examination of psychological theory, concepts, and methodology is enough to make plain the close ties between the science of psychology and religious doctrine. Religion's concern with the base versus the higher nature of man has been translated into psychology's concern with biological and second-order drives, id and superego, rationality and irrationality. The malleability and weakness of man's nature have given rise to an exploration of the conditioning contingencies of reinforcement, the "law of effect," and so on. The doctrine of predestination and preordination is mirrored in the psychological view of man as a passive recipient of either external (Skinner) or internal (Freud) forces, the unending circularity of the "nature-nurture" issue, the doctrine of the past determining the present, and the rejection of teleological concepts such as will and intention. The fall of man characterized in earlier times as a function of man's evilness and wickedness, the handiwork of demons and devils has become instead psychopathology, psychoses, criminality, and mental deficiency, concepts that have a more respectable place in the modern world. The priests' and rabbis' functions have largely been taken over by therapists, and those of the new prophets and later-day saints by the researchers and theorists in psychology. The mission of psychology has been made explicit by people as diverse as Maslow and Skinner. Maslow (1967) has unabashedly extolled humanistic psychology for fulfilling the functions that all organized religions throughout the ages have tried to fulfill. Skinner (1971) accepts the burden of the church, of the government, and other cultural institutions upon discovering how dismally they have served man. A new culture, one designed by behavioral scientists, must be instituted if man as a species is to survive. In a rare moment of insight, Skinner tied in his own religious childhood background with his conception of man: "I was taught to fear God, the police, and what people will think." He suspects that he may have reacted by trying to prove that people do not think at all (Harris, 1971).

It is no accident, then, that psychology has flourished in those countries that abandoned either a national church or God, especially in times of social and political chaos. The functions once served by a church—to offer explanations of catastrophic events, to provide prescriptions for behavior, to correct and punish offensive conduct (or thoughts)—have been taken over by psychology. While religion required a modicum of belief and a modest economic donation, psychology exacts a higher price with respect to both.

Thus, psychology moved into the vacuum created by the absence of a religious institution that could be counted upon to effectively foster the interests of the state. Even in countries with a national church, historical accounts (see Foucault, 1965; Sarbin, 1967; Merton, 1967) show that as the church weakened in its usefulness, the science of psychology and its ideological ally, psychiatry, gained in strength.

Psychology and Politics

The impact of politics on science has of late become a topic of increasing concern to observers of, and participants in, the scientific enterprise (see Blissett, 1972; Greenberg, 1967; Haberer, 1972). In a penetrating analysis of politicalization in science, Haberer (1972) suggests that scientists have adopted a stance, advocated over 300 years ago by Bacon, of "prudential acquiescence" in their relations with the ruling powers: "Their theories and their conduct posited retreat or an apparent acquiescence as the appropriate response to any serious confrontation with state or church." He indicates, further, that science, contrary to generally held assumptions, has often succumbed to parochial, nationalistic, political considerations.

Indeed, after observing first-hand the relative ease with which many scientists were transformed into the handmaidens of Nazi Germany, Ernst Krieck commented: "In the future, one will no more adopt the fiction of an enfeebled neutrality in science than in law, economy, the State or public life generally. *The method of science is indeed only a reflection of the method of government*" (in Merton, 1967; italics ours).

In their formative as well as later years, the natural sciences were interwoven in the economic and political fabric of society. Merton (1967) analyzed these influences upon the selection of scientific problems by the members of the Royal Society of London in the seventeenth century. The results showed that political (martial) and economic interests of the nation accounted for most of the research during that period (marine transport, military technology, mining, textile industry). Once the scientists were able to illustrate the usefulness of their techniques by obtaining practical results, they were then able (with the public's and the Crown's blessings) to turn to pure research.

As history unfolded, scientists were called by their nations many times to engage in needed practical research, to develop economic and military technologies. The Manhattan Project is, of course, just one example. Scientists in general, however, view with disdain practical research, attested to by the low status assigned to applied research. For instance, Jonas Salk, the inventor of the polio vaccine, was denied membership in the National Academy of Sciences presumably because he was not the first to kill viruses. That he applied this tissue culture technique in a socially beneficial and a creative way carried no weight with the "pure" scientists of the Academy. Indeed, the bind that pure scientists find themselves in, the need at times to engage in applied research even though they dislike it, has given rise to political in-fighting and intrigues worthy of the Borgias (see Greenberg, 1967).

With respect to the social sciences, Myrdal (1969) declares that: "Indeed, no social science or particular branch of social research can pretend to be 'amoral' or 'apolitical'. . . Research is always and by logical necessity based on moral and political valuations. . ." The evidence of "political conditioning" in the social sciences suggested by Myrdal (1969) is "the fact that it rarely blazes the way towards new perspectives. The cue to the continual reorientation of our work has normally come from the political interests that dominate the society in which we live."

Thus, in recent years, we witnessed a sudden flurry of scientific research activity directed toward racially linked diseases, the poor, mental retardation, compensatory education for the young, population control, violence, and so on, as a consequence of both personal and political interests of our national leaders.

There is, of course, nothing intrinsically wrong with doing research that derives from "political interests that dominate the society in which we live." As Myrdal (1969) points out: "The political conditioning of the direction of our work may simply be a rational way of adjusting it to the needs felt in the society in which we live and work." Research in sickle cell anemia, pollution control, and transportation systems could vastly improve the quality of all of our lives. In keeping with this political conditioning, the official purpose of the Amercian Psychological Association is to "advance psychology as a science, and as a means of *promoting human welfare*" (italics ours).

In a homogeneous society, or a totalitarian one, the political interests may be said to be isomorphic with human welfare. That is, what's good for the state is good for the individual.

In this context the role of the psychologist or social scientist is rather simple—he must merely translate the goals of the state into social action. Psychiatric reprisal, an excellent example of the political use of psychological concepts and techniques, has been known in the Soviet Union since the days of Peter the Great. In 1721, he empowered the senate with the right to determine the mental fitness of citizens. Thus, one Russian man, when it was learned that he participated in the French Revolution, was put in a lunatic asylum, the decree reading: "Whereas he did conduct himself as a madman, as a madman he shall be punished" (in Medvedev & Medvedev, 1971).

Today in the Soviet Union, with a more sophisticated citizenry and with an ear for public relations, psychiatric reprisal has been placed in the hands of the Serbsky Institute of Forensic Psychiatry, where experts conduct "special examinations" in order to determine the sanity of persons. Thus, a widely respected Russian biochemist, Zhores Medvedev, after publishing in the West an article offensive to some people in power in Russia, found himself in a nightmare of abduction, incarceration in a mental institution, and a psychiatric committee diagnosis of "incipient schizophrenic with paranoid delusions of reforming society" (see Medvedev & Medvedev, 1971).

In heterogeneous societies, those with pluralistic political systems and diverse, polarized interest groups, the role of the psychologist is not so clear-cut. Perhaps that explains why so many psychologists do little that could remotely be judged on traditional moral or political criteria. In any case, those few who attempt research in politically "loaded" areas face difficulties created by their inability or reluctance to make explicit their own moral stand. Thus, biases enter unnoticed into the formulation of the hypotheses, the selection of data to be used, the collection of the data, and the interpretation of the results.

For instance, one of the most controversial areas in psychology concerns racial differences in intelligence. Depending upon one's bias, research can be found to support either position; in other words, the results, or at least their interpretation, have led to antipodal conclusions—Negroes are innately inferior in intelligence to Caucasions or Negroes are not innately inferior to Caucasians.

In order to shed some light on this phenomenon, Friedrichs (1971) sampled several hundred members of the American Psychological Association to determine whether they agreed or disagreed with the Jensen theory of intelligence (that genetic factors are responsible for lower IQ scores obtained by Negroes). Friedrichs hypothesized that since psychology attracts people who "view man as relatively flexible in potential behavior," most should disagree. This was, in fact, the case. Sixty-eight percent disagreed with Jensen's theory. More revealing, however, were the results concerning factors that should have no influence on a "value-free" scientific judgment: age and geographic residence. Specifically, psychologists who lived in Alabama and Mississippi agreed more with Jensen than those who lived elsewhere, and those psychologists who disagreed with Jensen were about five years younger than those who agreed.

A more direct study of the social psychology of racial research was conducted by Sherwood and Nataupsky (1968), who examined the biographical data of 82 psychologists who had conducted research in the area of race and intelligence. They found that investigators whose research indicated that blacks were innately inferior to whites in intelligence tended to be the youngest of the sample when they published their study, were frequently first-born, third-generation (at least) Americans, with parents who had more education than the other groups in the sample, were raised in rural communities as children, and attained the highest scholastic records as undergraduates. In general, they came from higher socioeconomic backgrounds than the other researchers. Those investigators whose research indicated environmental differences between blacks and whites were the oldest when their research was published, were later born, had mothers with the lowest level of education, and, in general, were very different from the former group. The researchers who reported either no differences or variable differences clustered on the biographical items somewhere between the two extremes. That the authors demonstrated that *biographical data could be used to predict research conclusions,* illustrates the lack of independence or autonomy of the researcher, and the inability of his scientific methodology to exclude social forces from interfering with his research.

If we return, for a moment, to the view of the psychologist presented in Chapter One, these research findings though disconcerting are not surprising. To reiterate briefly, the psychologist, regardless of the posture he may assume, can function only in the role of scientist-as-moralizer. His attempts to enact the roles of technician, mediator, and purist can be viewed as disguises or evasions of his moral stance. As Gouldner (1962) remarks, the notion that social science should and, indeed, could be free of values is a myth created by Max Weber: "Like Berkeley's argument for solipsism, Weber's brief for a value-free sociology is a tight one and, some say, logically unassailable. Yet it is also absurd. For both arguments appeal to reason but ignore experience."

The similarity between religious doctrine and psychological concepts has already been illustrated. Political doctrine, though more diverse than the religious, as well as economic doctrine has also found its parallels in psychological theory. The basic concept of majority rule is reflected in the weight assigned to the nomothetic as opposed to the idiographic approach, the statistical definition of mental health, normal intelligence, and so on. The need of government to organize and control the populace is intertwined in psychology's preoccupation with mastery—that is, prediction and control of behavior; the ego (government) versus the id (masses); behavior modification. Incarceration because one violates the law is amplified by psychologists to include incarceration because of violating social norms. All men are created equal is mirrored by the tabula rasa theme. Even the political banners and slogans of the left and right are promoted by the humanists and the behaviorists. The law of the market, dynamic equilibrium is akin to psychic economy, homeostasis; wages to reinforcements; savings and surplus to delay of gratification and the reality principle; industrial specialization to psychological differentiation; the stick-and-carrot theory of labor is identical to reinforcement theory;

the manufacturing process of in-put, thru-put, and out-put is the basis of most psychological models such as S-O-R, psycho-cybernetics, and information theory.

Indeed, the intrusion of the marketplace mentality into the social sciences under the guise of the value-free doctrine (laissez-faire economics) has been remarked upon by Gouldner (1962). In his quotation, one may readily substitute psychology for Gouldner's reference to sociology.

> . . . the value-free doctrine is useful both to those who want to escape *from* the world and to those who want to escape *into* it. It is useful to those young men, or not so young men, who live off sociology rather than for it, and who think of sociology as a way of getting ahead in the world by providing them with neutral techniques that may be sold on the open market to any buyer . . . the market in which they vend their skills is unlimited . . . In brief, the value-free doctrine of social science was sometimes used to justify the sale of one's talents to the highest bidder and is, far from new, a contemporary version of the most ancient sophistry. (p. 212)

In this context, then, it is not surprising to find striking similarities between economic doctrine and psychological theory. After all, if one's own professional scientific conduct is determined by material reinforcements, why not the behavior of the rest of mankind?

To indicate parallelism in doctrine is not, of course, proof of the power of one discipline over the other. That is not our intention; instead, we merely wish to illustrate the similarity and suggest the ties that exist between psychology and theology, politics, and economics—a relationship more real than the spurious one psychologists have chosen to present to the public, which is the relationship between psychology, philosophy, and the natural sciences.

Psychology and Every Day

Even the realm of day-to-day activity of the psychologist has been totally neglected. As an ongoing process, it would seem that the most obtuse psychologist should recognize its potential as, at least, a partial determinant of his behavior. Skinner takes notes daily and records his ideas in order to keep the record straight (*Time*, September 20, 1971). Though his intent is similar, his account and analysis is no doubt different from that presented by Gouldner (1970) for the typical, tenured academic sociologist:

> For the tenured faculty, the university is a realm of congenial and leisured servitude. It is a realm in which the academician is esteemed for his learning but castrated as a political being. Indeed, it is this trade-off, in which the academician has the right to be a tiger in the classroom but the need to be a pussycat in the Dean's office, that contributes so much to the irrational posturing and theatrics of the classroom. Like other academics, the Academic Sociologist learns from the routine experience of his dependency within the university that he can strike terror only in the hearts of the very young—and now they want to strip him of even that privilege—but that he himself is the *gelded servant of the very system in which he is,* presumably, *the vaunted star.* He has thus learned with an intuitive *conviction that "society shapes men" because he lives it every day; it is his autobiography objectified.* (pp. 440–441; italics ours)

Many younger academicians, particularly sociologists and psychologists, realizing this aspect of university life, have rebelled against the academic establishment. Their "radical" attempts at achieving self-esteem (e.g., raising voices and fists at student and faculty meetings, refusing to participate in the assignment of grades to their students, assuming the posture of "guru" rather than professor) are empty gestures that obscure rather than confront the crises in academia.

It is intriguing, indeed, that the literature in sociology contains many insightful, self-critical analyses of the profession ranging from its theory and methods to the daily life of its practitioners, while psychology has not at all dealt with these issues in the same systematic way. This is not to say that psychology does not have its in-house critics, but rather that its critics somehow avoid the political, economic, and religious domain. As Myrdal (1969) notes, "scientists in any particular institution and political setting move as a flock, reserving their controversies . . . for matters that do not call into question the fundamental system of biases they share."

One could, of course, suggest that sociology's self-flagellation is merely a neurotic symptom born of the lack of necessary "epistemological sophistication," which enables the empirical scientist to realize that his symbolic and overt behaviors do not lie on the same methodological level as the behaviors of his subjects (Bergmann & Spence, 1944). Imagine the self-inflicted pain sociologists could have avoided had Bergmann and Spence been sociologists instead of psychologists.

In any case, psychology so far has been successful in stamping out or ignoring attempts at threatening criticism from within. Will it be as effective, however, in squelching criticism from outside the field?

The psychologist, in his role as moralizer, has aligned himself with the mainstream of society. Until recently, he was allowed to go about his activities unhampered, since those activities (see Chapters Five and Six) served the interests of the mainstream. But as the priorities shifted and the values and mores of society changed, psychology lagged behind, unable to decipher (since it is after all considered irrelevant to the psychological enterprise) the new public mandate. Attacks from outsiders have usually been viewed by psychologists as "ritualistic, bearing a striking resemblance to the territorial attack of howler monkeys," and as coming from the anti-intellectuals with whom we must bear (see Little, 1972). Of late, however, friends have begun to question seriously the job psychology is doing. This has resulted in some sober and intense self-questioning.

For instance, in response to the criticism of psychology in the field of corrections made by Judge David L. Bazelon, a "staunch friend of the behavioral and social sciences," Kenneth B. Little (1972), Executive Officer of the American Psychological Association, had this to say:

Public funds involve a public trust and Bazelon's critique is a symptom that the public may be beginning to wonder whether or not that trust has been violated . . . When he calls us to account, I personally get nervous for he does so on behalf of 204 million people. The most frequent question asked of APA by discontented members is: What do we get for our money? Consider the prospect of those 204 million people asking that question of psychology as a whole . . . I suspect that for the most part we are simply unprepared rather than unable to answer what the public wants to know: What is psychology good for? This means that we must scrutinize, assess, and structure our knowledge and skills appropriately to the task of convincing ourselves and reassuring the public . . . It will require soul-searching and liberal doses of our own methodological medicines but I think we can do it. (p. 2)

Searching the Soul of Psychology

The procedure we will follow includes an analysis of what psychology "knows," what it pretends to know, and what it is totally ignorant of. Myrdal (1969) has provided, in fact, the hypothesis and procedure for this study of the psychological enterprise:

> The hypothesis is that we almost never face a random lack of knowledge. Ignorance, like knowledge, is purposefully directed . . . If the degree of knowledge and ignorance and also their location and concrete character were analyzed . . . the valuations and their conflicts could be recorded indirectly but quantitatively . . . (p. 29)

In order to conduct the search, we must return to the embarrassing definition, "psychology is what psychologists do." That is, we will examine psychology in terms of the theories and methodologies it produces, the research it conducts, and the applications it performs. In addition, the social psychological implications for both the mainstream and marginal (surplus) populations it theorizes about, researches, and services will be explicated. The organization and analysis are schematically represented below.

We have, in part, already begun the search by examining the general relationship between psychology and the social institutions of religion, government, and economics. Though our

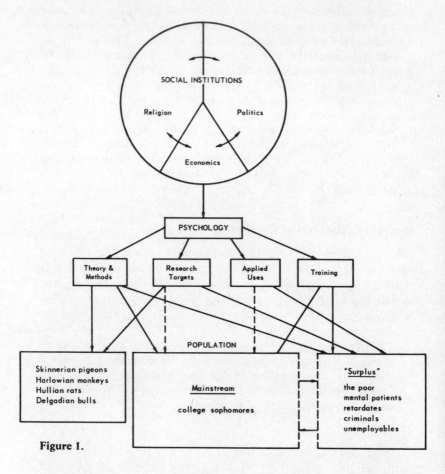

Figure 1.

treatment was admittedly brief, in the chapters that follow the relationships will be more precisely and probingly detailed. Before we leave the general ties between psychology and social institutions, a few more words concerning Figure 1 are in order.

The line between the social institutions and psychology is unidirectional; there is no representation of psychology's effect on these institutions. Thus, as pictured here, psychology today is an outcome of the forces that created and continue to shape it, having no autonomous existence, much less an influence upon these forces. One might suggest that this is an unfair or erroneous description. Instances might be cited of the role psychologists have played as expert witnesses on policy-making government agencies and in Supreme Court decisions, in addition to their services on national investigatory teams. Surely their efforts have had an impact upon governmental decisions.

Our reply to this may be gleaned from the previous pages. We know by now that some psychologists could somewhere be found who will lend credence to *any* point of view. Their participation, therefore, is nothing more than an attempt to clothe in scientific justification a policy decision that has already been made. The Supreme Court, though it reported social science research in its school integration decision, knew that it must desegregate schools in America; that the Constitution could not be violated any longer without our being prepared to pay an enormous sociopolitical price. Lyndon Johnson, while waging his "war on poverty," did not need psychological experts to tell him that ghetto children require compensatory education, poor people are malnourished, and malnutrition adversely affects the hungry child's ability to learn.

Indeed, the expectations of those who call on "experts" for policy advice and the ritualistic quality of the experts' performance are most obvious when the advice turns out to be unexpected and the ritual violated. The national uproar following the release of the pornography commission's report, which concluded that pornography does not cause an increase in sexual activity or perversion, illustrates just what happens when the "experts" do not give the anticipated responses. Their conclusions are ignored and denigrated by those who requested the study. Let us proceed now in the search by examining, if not the soul, then the very heart of psychology; that is, its theory and research methods.

THREE

Method and Theory – The Heart of Behaviorism

As we have previously noted, psychology is difficult to define or to even describe in a single meaningful way. Yet, there exist certain themes or approaches that encompass much of the psychological enterprise of today. These themes are represented by the antipodal approaches of the behaviorist movement and the humanist movement. Surely, there are many intermediary positions along this continuum, but we will not deal directly with these approaches, since none have had the impact, the mass appeal, or fired the imagination of psychologists in the same way as the behaviorist and the humanist movements.

Weekly magazines, newspapers, television shows, movies, and even books have been devoted to some very likely applications of these approaches: encounter, sensitivity, T or other groups, and utopian visions of a better world. Even the Guggenheim Museum has presented Esalen-type theater, where the actors squeezed, fondled, kissed, and rocked audience members in the name of living art.

Naturally, psychologists may argue that the public has

perverted, or at least distorted, the theories put forth by both the behaviorists and the humanists. This, no doubt, has some credence. In order to dispel any distortions that might have occurred, and to get on with our exploration of psychology, we will, in the following pages, closely examine present-day behaviorism and, in the next chapter, explore humanism in the context of the psychological enterprise. Since behaviorism is, by far, the mainstream of American psychology, particularly in the academic world (and gaining advocates daily in the clinical realm), and since the humanist movement is primarily a reaction against behaviorism, we will first deal with the methodology, theory, and language of behaviorism. The path we take has been illuminated by Myrdal (1969):

> The method of detecting biases is simple although somewhat laborious. When the unstated value premises of research are kept hidden and for the most part vague, the results contain logical flaws. When inferences are controlled with premises, there is found to be a *non sequitur* concealed, leaving the reasoning open to invasion by uncontrolled influences from the valuation sphere. (p. 54)

The Behaviorist Movement

The definition of psychology as the scientific study of *behavior* is the foundation of the behaviorist movement. That it is the most widely offered definition of psychology indicates how embedded behaviorism is in American psychology. In behaviorism, the psyche, the mind; and consciousness have been left to the philosophers, discarded because they cannot be observed. Watson (1913), the founder of behaviorism, stated that "the time has come when psychology must discard all reference to consciousness." From that time behaviorism flourished, proceeding, as Koch (1969) noted, "through eras of 'classical' behaviorism, neo-behaviorism, deflated neo-behaviorism, 'liberalized' neo-behaviorism, 'subjective' neo-behaviorism" to its present embodiment in Skinnerian behaviorism. These various movements, however, have not altered behaviorism's basic ideas, which can still be found in Skinner's (1971) recent charge to psychologists:

We can follow the path taken by physics and biology by turning directly to the relation between behavior and the environment and *neglecting supposed mediating states of mind* . . . We do not need to try to discover what personalities, states of mind, feelings, traits of character, plans, purposes, intentions, or the other prerequisites of autonomous man really are in order to get on with a *scientific analysis of behavior.* (p. 15; italics ours)

Related to the assertion of "down with the mind" is "up with the prediction and control" of behavior. That is, within the ideology of behaviorism is the belief that the task of psychology is to learn how to predict and then control the behavior of human beings as well as lower forms of life. Thus, the concept of prediction and control determines the shape of the behaviorist's psychological experiment, and, noting the enormous impact behaviorism has on the entire field of psychology, even nonbehaviorist research takes a similar form.

A basic assumption of behaviorism is that all organisms, including human beings, are passive and inert, moved into action and shaped solely by environmental forces. Therefore, neither man nor mouse can determine his own destiny. Since the metaphysical underpinnings of this assumption seem to be obvious to all but the behaviorists, they maintain that any idea that contradicts this "scientific" postulate is nothing more than a primitive myth that has long outlived its utility.

Another assumption of behaviorism is that once an organism is under the stimulation of the environment, it behaves in a way that will decrease any state of tension caused by either environmental or biological factors. Simply, then, organisms, regardless of their position in the phylogenetic scale, are tension-reduction automata.

The world of behaviorism is one of equality, where all living organisms are equally inert, passive, and susceptible to the tenets of prediction and control. The research strategy that follows from this view is that the scientist must first design an environment where the stimulus factors are controllable, observable, and quantifiable. In addition, the responses selected for study must share these attributes. These assumptions have led to a series of consequences, not only for psychology, but for society in general. For the present, however, we will only be concerned with the effects of behaviorism upon research in psychology and its theoretical ramifications.

Since its introduction, behaviorism has elicited either strong approval or strenuous disapproval among psychologists, but now it has become a veritable battleground. Skinner, the present-day embodiment of behaviorism, has been the object of deification by some and outrage by others. He, as well as all behaviorists, has been attacked not only by colleagues but by theologians, philosophers, humanists, politicians, and others who are familiar with the philosophy, political ramifications, and actual or desired applications of Skinnerian behaviorism. The critiques have dealt primarily with political and philosophical matters, never questioning the scientific validity of behaviorism (for one notable exception see Margolis, 1972).

The activities of the behaviorists have been legitimized by their rigorous exercise of the "scientific method." By now, it should be clear that just as a Steinway grand piano does not assure a well-executed piece, neither does the "scientific method" assure the acquisition of knowledge. Indeed, the worship of and the magical qualities attributed to the scientific method—methodolatry—have led the behaviorists to counter any and all arguments with the cry, "Look how much research this theory has generated." But as Koch (1969) cautions, "For those who would argue that the behaviorisms have nevertheless been richly productive of research should be reminded that *research is not knowledge*."

In this chapter, then, we will examine behaviorism's scientific and intellectual deficits, leaving for later chapters its applications and its impact upon political and philosophical issues.

The Methodolatry of Behaviorism

The only legitimate avenue of inquiry for psychologists who maintain the belief system previously described is to study units of behavior that are constructed and generated by researchers in a controlled experimental environment. In this environment, behavior is not examined from the point of view of the organism who is behaving (i.e., how he or it feels about what he or it is doing; how he or it interprets his or its own behavior, etc.) or from the social context in which the organism is interacting (i.e., the social forces that are present in the interaction between the researcher and his subject). These considerations must, of course, be dismissed when the experimenter is using animals as his subjects, since there is no way to determine these phenomena in nonspeaking organisms. Nonetheless, generalizations are made from these animals to human beings, making irrelevant the questions of context and personal meaning. In any case, the only *meaning* the behavior is allowed to have and the only social *context* considered is that which the experimenter creates. This selective process makes the behaviorist model of research particularly vulnerable to biases, misrepresentations of reality, and, therefore, most likely to generate pseudoknowledge and myths.

It must be emphasized here that the behaviorists are not alone in their endorsement of this research model. Many psychologists, though they avoid the formal aspects of behaviorism, employ this very limited perspective in their research. Festinger and Katz (1953), social psychologists, have described the "ideal" psychological experiment in a similar way:

> A laboratory experiment may be defined as one in which *the investigator creates a situation* he wants to have and in which *he controls* some, *and manipulates* other, *variables.* He is then able to measure the effect of the manipulation of the independent variables on the dependent variables in a situation in which the operation of other relevant factors is held to a minimum. (p. 137; italics ours)

This definition of the laboratory experiment tells us a great deal about the experimenter's construction of "reality," as well as his basic assumptions about the "nature" of the human situation. The description offered by Festinger and Katz, then, is not one of what actually exists; instead, it represents what psychologists think exist (i.e., their personal valuations and ideological constructs). Moreover, this description portrays the experimenter as a very busy person, manipulating environmental forces while observing the subjects' responses. The investigator, no doubt, would agree that this is an accurate depiction—we feel, however, that something is lacking. In order to complete the picture, an examination of a representative piece of research will be instructive. The research to be scrutinized is not singled out because it represents the worst in experimental strategy, but because it is, in fact, an excellent example of the best in research methodology.

It was noted by many researchers that animals respond more vigorously during early extinction trials than during the end of a reinforced series. Specifically, this means that if an animal has received over a number of trials a food pellet for depressing a lever, and if the food pellet suddenly does not appear when the lever is pressed, the animal will press the lever with even greater force. Three hypotheses were proposed by various authors in order to explain this observation: (1) nonreinforcement following the reinforcement series leads to frustration, which increases the general drive level of the animal, resulting in heightened performance; (2) based on associative rather than motivational factors, the animals may have learned during the reinforcement series that they had to press hard on the lever to activate the food pellet apparatus; or (3) vigorous bar-pressing is an earlier habit to which the animal regresses when he is thwarted by nonreinforcement.

In order to resolve this conflict, Blixt and Ley (1968) pitted the three hypotheses against each other in the following experiment. Fifth- and sixth-grade boys were required to push a strain gauge monitored lever in order to receive reinforcement (M&M candies). Whenever the subjects pushed within the range of predetermined force, they received an M&M candy.

One group of Ss was initially trained to lever push under conditions in which reinforcement was contingent upon a relatively light-force push. After this response was established, reinforcement conditons were altered so that reinforcement was contingent upon a relatively heavy-force push. Following the establishment of this response, Ss were placed on an extinction schedule. A second group received the same training except that this group was initially trained to make heavy pushes and then trained to make light pushes. The frustration-drive hypothesis would predict that both groups should show an increase in force of responding on the first extinction trial following nonreinforcement, whereas the regression hypothesis would predict that the heavy-to-light group should show an increase in force but the light-to-heavy group should show a decrease in force (i.e., a return to a previously established mode of responding). The associative hypothesis, however, would predict that the light-to-heavy group should show an increase in force, but the heavy-to-light group should show a decrease (i.e., if a heavy press does not pay off, a lighter press should). (p. 127)

A measure of the force was electrically obtained and the reinforcers were delivered by a remote controlled modified rodent pellet dispenser. This experiment employed scientific procedures and scientific terms. Therefore, the verbatim description of the study was included so that we may later examine the peculiar use of language in psychology and some of the results of that language.

The findings of the study were clear: All experimental groups showed vigorous responses during the first few trials of the nonreinforcement (extinction) series. That is, when the boys did not receive an M&M candy after depressing the lever, they pressed harder than when they did receive candy. The authors concluded that "the present data are completely consistent with predictions derived from the frustration-drive hypothesis."

Here we have an excellent example of scientific research— empirical observations, operationalism, statistical generalization, and prediction and control. The experimenters created the kind of environment required to solve the problem to which they addressed themselves. The environmental manipulations were easily quantifiable and explicit, and the dependent variable—the behavior of the subject—was observable. The problem had a respectable history in the scientific psychological literature, and the methods they chose and the logic they followed were in keeping with scientific simplicity, directness, and objectivity. Yet, their conclusion (as all conclusions of this sort) at best misrepresents and distorts the observations. What have they omitted in their formulation?

At one time or another, all of us have deposited money

in a vending machine, attempting to buy gum, cigarettes, coffee, or other items. What typically happens when money is deposited and the expected product is not forthcoming is that the buyer repeats the process with more force (e.g., pushes or pulls the lever much harder). If this repeated vigor does not release the desired product, some buyers may even punch or kick the machine. Why? The most obvious explanation is that people assume that the coin machine is not operating properly, that it is jammed or something is loose. The additional exerted force is an attempt to overcome the apparent malfunction and to get what they anticipated. Thus, additional force is nothing more than a rather reasonable response to a situation that leaves very little else to do. On this basis alone, it is quite possible to expect that the fifth- and sixth-grade boys exerted more force on the lever when the M&M candies did not come out in order to rectify an apparent malfunction of the dispensing machine. This simple and plausible explanation was never mentioned in the experiment. If it had been offered, the nature of the experiment would have been quite different. Very possibly, there would have been no experiment conducted at all, since there would be no problem in explaining why subjects "respond more vigorously during early extinction trials than during trials at the end of a reinforced series." That this possibility was never considered is instructive of what some experiments are about and what studies can do to "behavior."

It is noteworthy that no distinction was made between the original hypothesis based upon data compiled from rodents and the subsequent testing of that hypothesis on human subjects. Blixt and Ley (and their approach is typical of most studies in this area), without a word of explanation, chose fifth- and sixth-grade boys as an experimental population to test hypotheses based on rodent data. It is quite possible that rats also engage in "kicking the machine to unjam it," but we do not know, because we cannot ask the rats whether they have acquired the same knowledge as subway riders who use vending machines. We can, however, talk to fifth- and sixth-grade children and ask them why they pushed harder on the machine. The experimenters did not ask the boys this question, since they used the same experimental principles that were applied to the rats; that is, only observed behavior was recorded. More important, if an experimenter rejects the concept of human intelligence, thought, and creativity, then these factors cannot enter either into the design of his experiment, the questions he asks, or the answers he postulates. In short, experiments, quantification, and observable responses of subjects are no protection against the production of myths.

Since experiments are simply the constructions of researchers, a well-designed study is simply an experiment that fits the ideological stance of a particular group of researchers. If this stance is erroneous, misleading, or absurd, the results of the study will reflect these intellectual shortcomings. By and large, physical scientists have been saved from producing absurdities, not because they are more intelligent than psychologists, but because of the nature of the phenomena they investigate. If a physical scientist makes an error, it is probable that nothing will occur in his experiment. For example, if he postulates that X should happen, but X does not exist, then it will not appear. In the behavioral sciences, where an experimenter is dealing with complex, responsive, and plastic organisms, some behavior will inevitably occur, especially if you shock a subject or supply only one alternative for escaping the shock. Therefore, psychologists always obtain *something* from their subjects, while chemists or physicists may at times simply get no results. The psychologist, however, can observe an ambiguous bit of behavior, making it quite possible to conclude almost anything one wants to from the data.

The ambiguity of behavior is an extremely important element to consider in experiments. If we simply focused on a person's directly observable physical acts while ignoring what that person thought and felt about what he was doing, the context in which it occurred, and the observer's particular role and biases, we would know very little about the meaning of the behavior. For instance, if we observed a man raising his arm above his head with his fist clenched, failing to take into account the social context and what the person thought he was doing, all we would know is that a person had raised a clenched fist above his head. If, however, we took the personal and social contexts into account, we might discover that it was a salute to another person who belongs to the same political party, or that it was a gesture of defiance toward another person, or that he simply wanted to stretch.

By ignoring behavioral contexts, we reduce the amount of information related to the behavior and, thus, increase its ambiguity. Since most people depend on accurate information in order to adapt successfully to the world, they rely upon the contexts of every-day situations to give meaning to the behavior of others. Behaviorists, on the other hand, by the very design of their experiments, have pulled behavior out of naturally occurring contexts, narrowing the possibility of ever acquiring accurate information about that behavior. Their experimental constructions succeed only in increasing the ambiguity of behavior, which, for the behaviorists, represents an advantage. Since ambiguity does not aid understanding, it conveniently allows the researcher to shape what he sees into what he believes. Thus, a sixth-grade boy pushing a lever is simply seen as a "lever response" rather than how the boy sees himself: "I am pushing this silly lever for a piece of candy that I don't even like because I don't want to hurt the feelings of that nice man who thinks this is so important." Or when the sixth-grade boy, after receiving no M&Ms for several trials, stops pressing the lever, the experimenter sees this as "extinction." It might well be, taking varying contexts into account, a very different response (e.g., "The nice man who has been giving me those candies is losing interest, and, besides, the machine seems to be broken. Now, thank goodness, I can stop pressing this silly lever.") Thus, anything and everything is possible in these kinds of experiments simply because their design increases ambiguity.

If human behavior is made so difficult to understand by the behaviorists, what can we expect to discover when dealing with an organism with whom we cannot hope to communicate or share experiences? Obviously, the use of animals is the "ideal" strategy to increase ambiguity beyond all limits and to decrease any possibility of "meaningful" behavior. Thus, whether the subject is man or mouse, he is left out of the researcher's construction of reality, participating only as a passive recipient of experimental manipulations to which he responds.

Since he is of no consequence in the experimenter's formulation, the subject is not seen as a significant dimension in the interactions that occur in the laboratory setting. In the study we reported, no mention was made of the person-as-subject, but instead the fifth-grade boys could have easily been replaced by rats. The only active individual in the situation, then, is the experimenter who, as Festinger and Katz (1953) noted, "creates a situation he wants to have."

The investigators in the above study chose to see chocolate candies as "reinforcers" of behavior, and there is nothing to prevent them from engaging in this personal construction of "reality." But does the subject see the chocolate candies as a reinforcer, as *the* stimulus that changes the probability of his response? Or does he respond by pressing the lever for reasons other than obtaining an M&M candy? The experimenter may see the experiment as the investigation of learning—the subject may view the experiment as how well the experimenter can teach. The experimenter may see an electrical shock as an "independent variable"—the subject might see it as the experimenter's sadism, something to be avoided. The experimenter may see the withdrawal from a grill producing an electric shock as "shaped behavior" or as a "stamped in stimulus-response connection"—the subject may view his withdrawal as a function of good sense. An experimenter may view a subject who goes along with a group decision as a conformist—the subject may see his response as cooperation. Whose construction of reality is correct? Psychologists, no doubt, must assume they are correct, since it is their construction of reality that defines the laboratory experiment.

It has become increasingly clear that even the most rudimentary laboratory experiments involving people or animals are far more complex than simply the behaviors studied by the investigator (see Orne, 1962; Rosenthal, 1966; Bakan, 1967). It is not accidental that the subject, especially when human, plays a subordinate role in the laboratory experiment. If one examines how people are typically seen and treated in the experimental situation, one *has* to delete them from any explanation of what occurs in the laboratory. First, people are called *subjects*. The popular definition of *subject* is one who is placed under the authority, dominion, control, or influence of another or something else. This definition states that a subject occupies a subordinate, somewhat powerless position in the social ecology. The meaning of subject held by social scientists is quite similar: "one who or that which is operated upon, experimented with, tested, studied, etc." This particular construction, however, leaves no room for the recognition of positive, active, manipulative, and imaginative attributes associated with being human.

The term subject, as it is applied to people used in experiments, becomes a key to understanding the constructs of psychologists irrespective of content; constructs that are relevant to the world of objects but not to people. When the psychologist sees people as subjects, he is not engaging in a semantic enterprise. To the contrary, when he labels people as subjects, he socially transforms them into "objects" and then treats them accordingly. For example, almost all studies involving people have in their design some method for keeping the subjects naïve about the experiment. Typically, this is accomplished by saying nothing to the subjects except for instructions (often "bogus") and by asking them only about things in which the experimenter is interested. The belief that the subject can be kept naïve fosters two important illusions for the experimenter: (1) the illusion that people are in fact objects, or noninteractive entities; and by forbidding interactions during the course of the experiment between investigator and subject, (2) the illusion that the experiment is controlled, simple, pure, and isolated from real life. Thus, the psychologist can feel as if he has successfully controlled intrusive and irrelevant variables—variables that taint field or naturalistic experiments.

Psychologists, however, are implicitly aware that if subjects were to know what the experimenters were doing, the results of the study would be different. That is, the hypotheses would not be borne out by the data because subjects might purposefully shift the responses away from the experimenters' expectations. Or, the hypotheses would be supported by the data because the subjects might wish to aid the experimenter by giving him the expected response. Orne (1962), as well as other psychologists, has produced evidence of this phenomenon. Thus, deeply embedded in the experimental strategy of keeping people naïve is the recognition that although subjects are treated, thought of, and described as objects, they are really people.

There are other reasons for the use of object language in the laboratory experiment. Some are political, economic, and social in origin, and we will discuss these later. We will focus here upon those reasons that are based upon psychologists' conceptions of the role and purpose of laboratory settings. It should be clear even to the beginning student in an experimental psychology course that laboratories are designed to *extract* information from subjects. Therefore, experiments are extractive situations, where the independent variables represent the devices of extraction, and the dependent variables represent what has been extracted. The *extractive* construction, when perceived as a reality, limits the psychologist to the artifacts that are embedded in this conception.

There are many ways to conceptualize people and their relationship to the world. The general conception views people as dynamic entities who are not simply shaped but who also shape, to some extent, their social environment. People *"give and take"*; it is a rare stiuation when one person has to extract something from another, and this usually occurs under coercive conditions—for example, when police have to extract a confession; a parent has to extract the truth from an unwilling child; a teacher has to extract the answer from a stubborn student. In these situations the target person (the unwilling member) acts *as if* he is an object, reluctant to participate in social intercourse. In this sense, the target person denies himself an important dimension of being human. It is no surprise, then, that the extractor (the parent, police, etc.) in these relationships fails to treat the object-like target as human (witness the use of "inhuman" extractive techniques such as torture).

The psychologist who creates a rather rare human condition (i.e., an extractive relationship) enters a very strange world, indeed. The scientist who purportedly wishes to establish general laws of human behavior, yet chooses to study rare behavior that occurs under very special conditions, is involved in an illogical, if not absurd, strategy. Furthermore, when dealing with human subjects, the extractive conception distorts even a nonexperimental reality. The psychologist usually conducts his research with people who *volunteer* for his study. It would seem that these people are willing to give the psychologist the information he requires. The psychologist thus works against himself by transforming a voluntary situation into an extractive relationship. Some psychologists, of course, might argue that people are either unwilling to share important information about themselves or are unable to do so. This argument, however, does not detract from this analysis of the laboratory experiment. This argument, in fact, affords more evidence that the person-as-subject is seen as an object to be manipulated and controlled in order to extract the information the scientist desires.

The depiction of the experiment as a stage setting, contrived by the investigator, where subjects are cast either as objects or infrahuman organisms, is supported by numerous stage techniques. The most effective device is the researcher's specialized use of language, which offers him a script to support his allusions of scientific objectivity and situational control, while, at the same time, it permits him to produce and transform ambiguous behavior into support for his hypotheses.

Hull (1943), a renowned experimental psychologist, recognized early the importance of language in the scientific enterprise:

> . . . one of the greatest obstacles to the attainment of a genuine theory of behavior is anthropomorphic subjectivism. At bottom this is because we ourselves are so intimately involved in the problem; we are so close to it that it is difficult to attain adequate

perspective . . . Even when fully aware of the nature of anthropomorphic subjectivism and its dangers, the most careful and experienced thinker is likely to find himself a victim of its seductions.

He proposed that the serious student of behavior employ the verbal and mental prophylaxis of thinking in terms of subhuman species, although this, too, is full of danger for the unwitting scientist:

Unfortunately this form of prophylaxis against subjectivism all too often breaks down when the theorist begins thinking what he would do if he were a rat, a cat, or a chimpanzee; when that happens, all his knowledge of his own behavior, born of years of self-observation, at once begins to function in place of the objectively stated general rules or principles which are the proper substance of science.

According to Hull, the best solution to the tacky problem of keeping one's own knowledge and experience out of one's scientific endeavors is to:

. . . regard from time to time the behaving organism as a completely *self-maintaining robot*, constructed of materials as unlike ourselves as may be . . . The robot approach thus aids us in avoiding the very natural but childish tendency to choose easy though false solutions to our problems, by removing all excuses for not facing them squarely and without evasion. (pp. 27–28; italics ours)

Surely Hull, or anyone for that matter, is free to choose whatever strategy he desires in the pursuit of knowledge. Nonetheless, the reasons Hull offers in support of this cognitive strategy are illogical. Hull does not suggest that people are really objects or robots. However, it is because people are not like robots, because they are human, that we must study them as if they were robots. What Hull argues is that we cannot get to know about people if we study them as people; instead we must study them as rodents, cats, or chimps; or better still, as mechanical objects. But this appears to be illogical. Obviously, if you were interested in finding out about fish and someone told you that to do so you should study wind-up toys, we think you would consider this advice, at the very least, peculiar.

In real terms, then, what Hull is offering the psychologist is a prophylaxis against understanding human behavior. If Hull's position is carried to its extreme (as Skinner has done), the ultimate language of psychology would be the language of the external environment, since even robots may have qualities reminiscent of human beings. Hull's contribution has been to make explicit the commandment that the psychologist, in order to be a *good* scientist, must substitute object language for subjective, anthropomorphic "people-language." Since our use of language shapes our conceptions of what we think is real, this has had many consequences. Let us now examine the metamorphosis of language at the hands of the behaviorists.

Behaviorist Jargon

Skinner (1971), in his most recent work, repeats the call that psychologists must move away from the antiquated, unscientific language of freedom and dignity and use in its place the language of scientific behaviorism. His rationale is that behaviorist language clarifies what really is happening rather than obscuring phenomenon with meaningless, ambiguous words. As an example of the clarity that comes from the uses of behaviorist terms, Skinner translates for us a common situation. First, we will present his translation (which, according to Skinner, is a more meaningful, less ambiguous scientific representation); then, we will ask the reader to try to explain what Skinner is describing; finally, we will present the subjective, antiquated description.

Consider a young man whose world has suddenly changed. He has graduated from college and is going to work, let us say, or has been inducted into the armed services. Most of the behavior he has acquired up to this point proves useless in his new environment. The behavior he actually exhibits can be described, and the description translated as follows: [here we provide only the translated description] . . . (his behavior is weak and inappro-

priate); . . . (he is seldom reinforced, and as a result his behavior
undergoes extinction); . . . (extinction is accompanied by emotional responses); . . . (his behavior frequently has unavoidable
aversive consequences which have emotional effects); . . . (he is
rarely reinforced for doing anything); . . . (he has previously
been punished for idleness or failure, which now evokes emotional responses); . . . (he is no longer reinforced by the admiration of others, and the extinction which follows has emotional
effects) . . .

Does this description denote anything, even to the most
stubborn proponent of behaviorism? Can anything that translates this poorly lead to the acquisition of understanding or
knowledge? Let us look at the source and the translation side
by side:

. . . he lacks assurance or feels insecure or is unsure of himself
(*his behavior is weak and inappropriate*); he is dissatisfied or
discouraged (*he is seldom reinforced and as a result his behavior
undergoes extinction*); he is frustrated (*extinction is accompanied by emotional responses*); he feels uneasy or anxious
(*his behavior frequently has unavoidable aversive consequences
which have emotional effects*); there is nothing he wants to do
or enjoys doing well, he has no feeling of craftsmanship, no
sense of leading a purposeful life, no sense of accomplishment
(*he is rarely reinforced for doing anything*); he feels guilty or
ashamed (*he has previously been punished for idleness or failure,
which now evokes emotional responses*); he is disappointed in
himself or disgusted with himself (*he is no longer reinforced by
the admiration of others, and the extinction which follows has
emotional effects*) . . . (p. 147)

For those who wish to learn the skills of translation into
behaviorist jargon, Ferster and Perrott (1968, p. 111) offer a
lesson in the form of a sample analysis of the following human
situation:

A group of children were playing in the playground. John
snatched a marble from Frank and ran away. Frank immediately
chased after him. When Frank caught him, Johnny put the

marble in his mouth. Frank sat on him on the ground, twisted his arm behind him and said, "Give me that marble." Tears came to Johnny's eyes before he finally spit out the marble and ran away.

A Sample Analysis

Original	*Translation*
1. A group of children were playing in the playground. John snatched a marble from Frank and ran away.	1. John's snatching the marble from Frank was the withdrawal of a positive reinforcer. John's running away was a performance maintained by escape from an aversive stimulus: Frank would take the marble and/or hit him if he stayed.
2. Frank immediately chased after him.	2. Frank: A performance maintained by positive reinforcement (in the past, running after people led to catching them). John: Avoidance; running prevented the aversive stimulus (loss of the marble and threat of a beating) so long as he ran fast enough.
3. When Frank caught him, Johnny put the marble in his mouth.	3. A further example of avoidance.
4. Frank sat on him on the ground, twisted John's arm behind him and said, "Give me that marble."	4. An aversive stimulus was supplied with an instruction that its termination depended on giving up the marble.
5. Tears came to Johnny's eyes before he finally spit out the marble and ran away.	5. Giving up the marble was reinforced by the termination of the aversive stimulus. The marble at this point was a positive reinforcer for all of Frank's behavior: Largely applying aversive stimuli. The aversive stimulus elicited reflexes.

It is obvious by now that these translations offer not only an inaccurate portrayal of the human situation but a peculiar one as well. Important information is excluded in the shift from words that denote human affairs to words that denote the objective realm of the value system of the observer. Indeed, any professional translator would never think of omitting the amount of information that is lost when one uses behavioristic translations. Not only is information lost by using object-language in place of people-language, but erroneous, distorted misinformation takes its place. Thus, statements like "the aversive stimulus elicited reflexes" or "his behavior has unavoidable aversive consequences" could represent almost any situation: a criminal being electrocuted, a mother punishing her child, a professor giving a student a failing grade.

Many behaviorists believe that this is, in fact, the goal of their translating activities. That is, to subsume a variety of diverse behaviors and situations with identical, objective terminology. They have obviously confused the production of a general language with one of the goals of scientific activity— to produce general laws. There is, of course, a difference between laws and language, particularly a language that has sacrificed meaning for generality. Asch (1959) describes what occurs when concepts such as response strength, conditioning, extinction, reinforcement and so on are extrapolated to social settings:

> The extrapolations become largely verbal; we are not the wiser when the translation has been accomplished. This procedure, instead of increasing objectivity, often conceals distinctions long familiar to ordinary observation. It discourages the exploration of those differences between persons and things, between living and dead, that are the center of the subject. It creates the curious presumption that hardly anything new remains to be discovered in a field that has barely been studied. (p. 378)

At best, then, the use of language appropriate to robots is ambiguous when applied to people and at worst leads to myths and illusions (see Sarbin, 1967). As Hull pointed out, reality does not suggest the use of object-language, but rather object-language is used because some psychologists have committed themselves to a particular reality predicated by an ideological stance called behaviorism. This language permits those psychologists who believe in behaviorism to see what they desire and to ignore or deny the existence of what they cannot fit into machine or object terms.

Methodolatry and Jargon

The experimental method in psychology can be reexamined as a *ritualized method for retranslating the human situation into a nonhuman one.* The experiment is the concrete manifestation of an ideological commitment to the nonhuman world. Experimental method as practiced by the behaviorists, and emulated by other kinds of psychologists, is, as we have already seen, a peculiar transforming device. It is no surprise, then, that the range of behaviors a subject is allowed in experimental situations is minimal and machine-like. Subjects are asked to press bars, buttons, and levers, to wear electrodes, and to point to stimuli—activities that can be easily duplicated (on a phenotypical level) by machines. Although complex behavior may occur during the experiment, the trained investigator is still able to focus on the designated behavior (e.g., reaction time, brain waves, frequency or forcefulness of bar presses).

Briefly, the marriage of behaviorism to the experimental method serves many purposes. Primarily, it helps to disguise the ideological stance of behaviorism, while, at the same time, it lends credence to the belief system that created it. That is, the language of behaviorism conveys scientific respectability, which, at first, obscures the logical flaws and the *non sequiturs* that Myrdal (1969) attributes to unstated, hidden value premises.

Although Myrdal warns that the process of uncovering the biases are laborious, Skinner has simplified the task. His reputation has been the result of clarifying his assumptions about man and the human condition. Skinner's explicit political and philosophical stance, in addition to his commitment to technological apparatuses, has unfortunately served to deflect attention from his scientific thinking. That is, the scientific productions (both research and theory) of behaviorism have gone unquestioned. Instead, the criticisms have been focused on the ramifications of their productions. An analysis of Skinnerian thought will indicate that the criticisms and alarm Skinner has aroused are unwarranted. There can be few ramifications of his work since Skinner's contributions to the knowledge of psychology have been minimal. It is because Skinner is considered so important to psychology, and because he is hailed by the American Psychological Association as "a pioneer in psychological research, leader in theory, master in technology, who has revolutionized the study of behavior," that we must offer this critique.

The Skinnerian Approach

Most people make distinctions between statements that can be tested and those that cannot or are not meant to be tested. For example, statements that cannot be tested include such assertions as, "I believe there is a God" or "Man is basically evil," and so on. Other assertions are recognized as nonsense; that is, they are not meant to be tested. There are a number of methods by which we can produce nonsensical statements, some of which are ingenious and charming (e.g., Edward Lear's nonsense verses) and others that are serious-minded and bleak.

Let us begin with a classical Skinnerian experiment involving a pigeon (Skinner, 1953). A hungry pigeon is placed in a Skinner box (an isolated, soundproof, highly controlled environment), where he is fed repeatedly from an electrically controlled tray. When the pigeon readily eats the food we are ready to begin "to make this consequence contingent upon behavior and to observe the result." The behavior, of course, must be easily observable and measurable. In the case of the pigeon, the raising of the head is a convenient behavior to observe. The experimenter, after carefully studying the normal height at which the pigeon holds his head, opens the food tray rapidly whenever the pigeon's head rises above a predetermined, atypical line. According to Skinner "the result is invariable; we observe an immediate change in the frequency with which the head crosses the line," provided (and this is an interesting stipulation) "the experiment is conducted according to specifications."

He bemoans the "explanatory fictions used to explain the process of stamping-in such as 'trial and error.'" Indeed, he feels that even the term "learning" is an inaccurate report of what is happening and is, therefore, misleading. The barest statement of this process for Skinner is: *"we make a given consequence contingent upon certain physical properties of behavior* (the upward movement of the head), and *the behavior is then observed to increase in frequency"* (italics ours).

Is this, in fact, the barest possible statement of the foregoing events? Skinner has presented us with a hungry pigeon and a person who feeds this pigeon every time the head is raised to a prescribed level. After a brief period, the pigeon keeps his head up to the norm established by the person, as long as the pigeon is fed. This seems to be a straightforward, simple situation. Skinner declares that we must not speak of these events in terms of learning, habit, trial and error, or any other concept that assumes an operation occurring *inside* the bird.

Since we cannot hope to know what, if anything, goes on inside the pigeon, it seems to make good sense not to assume the existence of some mental process. Creating "ghosts in the machine" can lead only to concepts like entelechy, soul, mind, and other unscientific notions. Thus, Skinner maintains that what transpired during the experiment was that a given consequence was made "contingent upon certain physical properties of behavior . . . ; and the behavior [was] observed to increase in frequency."

The description of events is simply a description of the notions inside the experimenter's head. "Food as a consequence" is a concept employed only by the feeder, unless Skinner is willing to concede that the bird cognizes consequences. But surely he would not engage in the very activities he criticizes. His statement of events, then, is a description of the phenomenology, the experience of "reality," of the investigator, and not a description of the experience of pigeons, of rodents, or of other men. "Food as a consequence" denotes only how Skinner and other behaviorists interpret what is occurring between them and their subjects.

If we were to employ the behaviorists' notion of modification of behavior to describe the events of the experiment, we would find that the pigeon's head-raising behavior is not the only behavior that increases in frequency—the feeding behavior of the experimenter also increases in frequency. An accurate description, therefore, of what occurs between man and pigeon must include the transactions that occur between the *two parties*, as well as the change in behavior of *both parties*. It is obvious that a change in the bird's behavior leads to a corresponding change in the behavior of the investigator. On what basis, then, does Skinner justify the exclusion of the modification of the experimenter's behavior from his interpretation of events in the laboratory?

Of course, the investigator may simply be interested in the pigeon and not in himself, but this cannot be used as an explanation when the problem, as Skinner sees it, is to describe with accuracy what is transpiring during the experiment. If we include both parties in our formulation, interesting questions arise. Specifically, are we perhaps looking at a man and a pigeon attempting to communicate and teach one another what is important to each of them? Does the hungry bird teach the experimenter that food is what he needs, while the experimenter teaches the bird that it is "height of head" that he needs? If this sounds strange, it is because, for the moment, we have accepted Skinner's descriptive statement. According to his logic, it is plausible to assume that the pigeon has effectively shaped the behavior of the experimenter by making the experimenter's response contingent upon the bird's own head-raising. This is no more peculiar than Skinner's depiction of events. It appears a bit ridiculous because we all are aware that people are smarter, stronger, and especially more controlling than birds. Using this assumption, it would be nonsense even to consider a pigeon shaping the experimenter's behavior. Skinner's description, therefore, makes sense only if we accept this hidden assumption. Even assuming that this is an accurate belief, it still does not follow that Skinner is correct in presenting a one-sided conceptualization of the events that transpired between man and pigeon. If his intention was to present the "barest possible statement of the process," he clearly failed. The barest statement might read: "hungry pigeon was fed every time he bobbed his head above a certain height. After a short time, his head remained at that height."

The proponents of behaviorism, indeed most scientists, would argue that this last statement is too concrete—that Skinner has abstracted out the theoretical properties of the events so that the scientific laws of behavior he has formulated may be demonstrated. To answer this and to explore what Skinner really is doing, let us first turn to the laws of behavior that he has formulated.

The Laws of Reinforcement and Extinction

Although they differ in many respects, almost every major learning theorist has verified the Law of Reinforcement and the Law of Extinction (see Guthrie, 1935; Hull, 1943; Miller, 1951; Mowrer, 1950; Spence, 1956). Briefly, the central theme of operant reinforcement theory is that behavior is influenced by the changes that occur in the environment as a consequence of that behavior. If the behavior results in favorable consequences, the principle of positive reinforcement is operating, which leads to an increase in the frequency of that behavior. On the other hand, if favorable consequences do not follow a particular behavior, the behavior occurs with less frequency. The Law of Extinction refers to the decrease in frequency of a behavior after the previously reinforced response is no longer reinforced.

Thus, any attempt to modify behavior is subsumed under these two laws, increasing the frequency of desired behavior or decreasing the frequency of undesired behavior. The major problem, then, that the behaviorist confronts is not how to change behavior but to discover reinforcers for the organism whose behavior is to be modified. What are reinforcers, then, and what special knowledge do behaviorists have to facilitate the formulation of reinforcers?

To discover reinforcers, as Ayllon and Azrin (1968)

point out, one must first take care not to confuse the terms "reward" and "reinforcer." Although many people use the terms interchangeably, we are reminded that "a difference between them exists which is *crucial for success in discovering effective human motivators*" (italics ours). The difference between rewards and reinforcers is believed to reflect the distinction between the *mentalistic* and the *behavioristic* approaches to human behavior.

Specifically, rewards indicate subjective states (i.e., pleasant or satisfying sensations) that, when attempting to specify what is rewarding, force the scientist to ask individuals, "What do you like or want?" "What symbolic significance does this have for you?" and so on. Ayllon and Azrin indicate the danger of carrying to its extreme the subjective endeavor to specify the phenomenological or subjective world of the individual—that is, "the mentalistic philosophy *minimizes the necessity for obtaining measures of behavior* upon which to base one's estimate of subjective likes or dislikes" (italics ours). This is indeed dangerous since it would eliminate the work (research) of the behaviorist whose job it is to obtain the measures of behavior in order to determine reinforcing stimuli.

Of course, when studying animals, one cannot ask for subjective reports. Nothing prevents the behaviorists, however, from querying human subjects, except for their aversion to verbal interchange of this sort, which we noted earlier. It is no surprise, then, to find that their term—reinforcer—requires no communication with the organism. That is, "the definition of reinforcer has its basis in its effect upon behavior." Or as Skinner (1953) puts it, "The only defining characteristic of a *reinforcing stimulus* is that it *reinforces*."

Although Skinner's definition appears tautological, he tells us shortly after presenting this statement that, "There *is nothing circular about classifying events in terms of their effects*; the criterion is both empirical and objective" (italics ours). In this simple manner, then, Skinner satisfies his followers and anticipates his critics by telling everyone that to define a reinforcing stimulus as that which reinforces is not circular.

For thousands of years man has struggled to break away from such primitive thinking. How did primitive people know that rain gods existed? Because it rained. Or of the existence of war gods? Because there were wars. In order to accept Skinner's notion, we would have to argue that the moon be defined by its influence on the earth's tides; feeding a starving man by the increase in his blood-sugar level; love by a kiss. Indeed, to accept Skinner's criteria of logic would be to place ourselves in a time-machine that would transport us back to the days when supernatural powers filled the world, and we would know them by their effects.

Skinner does suggest that were he to "assert that a given event strengthens an operant because it is reinforcing," it would be circular. But he does, in fact, say just this a short while after he denounced that very tautology. Specifically, if there is a change in the frequency of behavior, Skinner remarks, "we classify the event as *reinforcing* to the organism." Furthermore, he attributes the success "in guessing at reinforcing powers" to a kind of crude survey: *"We have gauged the reinforcing effect of a stimulus upon ourselves and assume the same effect on others"* (italics ours).

Thus, Skinner's denial of circular thinking and the example of what he considers circular are not assets to him. First, his definition is circular. Second, he engages in exactly what he presented as an example of circular reasoning. Specifically, he denies any effect embodied in the notion of reinforcement, yet a few lines later discusses the "reinforcing effect of a stimulus."

To complete this confusion, we return to the explanations Skinner so strongly rebukes. Assumed inner causes for changes in behavior, such as learning, incentive, habit, and so on, are replaced by Skinner's own behavioral formulations. For instance, to his own question "Why is a reinforcer reinforcing?" Skinner responds, "A biological explanation of reinforcing power is perhaps as far as we can go in saying why an event is reinforcing." Reinforcement is, after all, located somewhere inside the organism related to some as yet unknown, unspecified biological mechanism.

To illustrate further the absurdity of behaviorism, a structurally identical example of Skinner's reasoning, utilizing different terminology, follows.

Zog, Zoger, Zogment: The Paradigm

Professor X has discovered that he has certain powers over pigeons. To demonstrate these newly discovered powers, he creates a situation similar to Skinner's experiment (head-raising responses). After the demonstration, a psychology student asks Professor X, "What are you doing?" The professor replies that he is exercising his power by mastering and controlling the behavior of the pigeon. The student then asks, "Why is a busy man like you doing this? Are you interested in developing an animal act?" Professor X understandingly smiles and says, "I am developing a theory about my power to control this bird's behavior." "Oh, I see," replies the student, "but what exactly is going on between you and that pigeon?" The professor answers, "I am making a given consequence contingent upon certain physical properties of behavior." Impressed now with his professor, the student says: "Wow, sir. Well, why do you think the bird changes his behavior?" "The bird changes his behavior," replies the professor, "as a function of my power, which I call *Zog*." The student asks, "How do you define *Zog*?" To which the Professor responds, "By its effect, naturally." "But where is *Zog* located? In the food? In you? In the bird?" asks the student. Indeed, the puzzled student adds, "It can't be in the food because that would invest supernatural powers to food. It can't be in you since that would invest you with supernatural powers. Even if you did possess *Zogment* power, could you transfer it to the bird by means of the food? That's foolish. It can't be in the bird because that would mean the bird had *Zog* power and not you. Besides, how do *you know* if something has *Zogment* power?"

Professor X, somewhat annoyed by now, replies, "Whether or not you believe it, I have the power to *Zog*. All I need to know are the right conditions that must exist for my

Zoger to be effective. I know something has *Zogment* power when it *Zogs* and I know it *Zogs* if I was successful at changing the bird's behavior. I don't know in advance whether my *Zogment* power will work, but if those whom I direct it to change their behavior, I know then."

The student, confused and dejected, turns to leave the room. Professor X shouts after him, "You too might have *Zogment* power, but you will never know how to use it unless you allow me to teach you." The young student hurriedly goes to the academic dean in order to switch his major course of study.

If the hypothetical dramatization seems foolish, absurd, and magical, it is not because we spoke of *Zog* power instead of the power to *reinforce*, but rather because we have borrowed the beliefs and the logic of Skinnerian theory.

It is no surprise that Skinner and his followers have failed to respond fully to their critics. Indeed, Skinner (Rice, 1968) has said, "I never answer any of my critics. I generally don't even read them. There are better things to do with my time than clear up their misunderstanding." It is noteworthy that those very "commandments" of science Skinner articulated in 1953 (open-mindedness among them) are now violated by him when he describes his critics as neurotics, psychotics, and fools. Whenever behaviorists, although not Skinner, choose to reply, it usually reads: No matter what anyone says or thinks, the behavior of both animals and people is modified when they are in a Skinnerian setting. It works!

Is there evidence, then, that operant conditioning does, in fact, work? Breland and Breland (1961), both of whom were staunch supporters of Skinnerian behaviorism, summarize their years of research using this paradigm:

Our first report (Breland & Breland, 1951) in the *American Psychologist*, concerning our experiences in controlling animal behavior, was wholly affirmative and optimistic, saying in essence that the principles derived from the laboratory could be applied to the extensive control of behavior under non-laboratory conditions throughout a considerable segment of the phylogenetic scale. When we began this work, it was our aim to see if the science would work beyond the laboratory, to determine if animal psychology could stand on its own feet as an engineering discipline . . . However, in this cavalier extrapolation (from the Skinner box), we have run afoul of a *persistent pattern of discomforting failures*. These failures, although disconcertingly frequent and seemingly diverse, fall into a very interesting pattern. They all represent breakdowns of conditioned operant behavior . . . *After 14 years of continuous conditioning and observation of thousands of animals, it is our reluctant conclusion that the behavior of any species cannot be adequately understood, predicted, or controlled without knowledge of its instinctive patterns, evolutionary history, and ecological niche.* In spite of our early successes with the application of behavioristically-oriented conditioning theory, we readily admit now that ethological facts and attitudes in recent years have done more to advance our practical control of animal behavior than recent reports from American "learning labs" (pp. 681, 684; italics ours).

Nonetheless, as we shall see in later chapters, behavior modification systems are being set up in institutions across the United States. Those who have initiated these systems report remarkable success at behavior modification with respect to hospitalized mental patients, retardates, production workers, and even some college students. Ayllon and Azrin (1968) note that most parents *intuitively* use the principle of reinforcement with their children, industrialists with their production workers, therapists with their clients, and so on. The authors concede that the use of incentives is by no means novel. The problem encountered by nonscientists, however, is that "in practice rewards are usually intuitive, incidental, infrequent, often trivial, unstandardized, and given with little regard to their relationship to the rewarded performance."

It is nonsense to believe, however, that the scientists who gave M&M candies to fifth- and sixth-grade boys for pushing a lever were unencumbered by the difficulties cited above, whereas the industrialist who pays his employees, including bonuses at times, can never hope to be as effective at behavior control. Since the beginning of recorded history, human beings have been preoccupied with learning to control and master others. The success, in recent years, of politicians at mass behavior modification should make the behaviorist envious, indeed. Hitler succeeded in turning thousands of nice, god-fearing men into mass executioners. Madison Avenue agencies, without the benefit of Skinner, have succeeded in modifying the behavior of voters by manipulating the images of presidential candidates. The expert staff who succeeded in getting President Nixon elected, described by McGinnis (1969), included ghost writers, makeup men, set designers, and advertising specialists —but not one behavioristic psychologist. It might be argued, however, that whether they knew it or not, these successful behavior changers were employing the Laws of Reinforcement and Extinction. And this raises the final point in our analysis of behaviorist theory and research.

When behaviorists are successful in modifying behavior, it is not because they possess knowledge peculiar to themselves. Instead, they are successful only because they borrowed common knowledge, the knowledge of the marketplace, which has led to success for thousands of years. For example, Skinner, in 1938, showed us that our behavior is to a large extent determined by the consequences that follow. Thus, knowledge that is available to every person has been retranslated beyond recognition, embodied in an untestable, tautological, and contradictory "theory" and then passed off as new laws of behavior. Thus, "you get more bees with honey than with vinegar" becomes the central theme of positive reinforcement. "If you don't pay them, they won't work" becomes the Law of Extinction.

Neither the camouflage of jargon nor the respectability and arrogance of the "scientist" is enough to transform behaviorist morality into a scientific theory of behavior. The "Four Pillars of Unwisdom" ascribed by Koestler (1968) to behaviorism serve only to "scientize" the Protestant, capitalistic morality of our society-at-large. Thus, under Skinner's cloak of scientific respectability we may return to a "modern version of the Dark Ages" (Koestler, 1968) where man can be exploited, degraded, and duped in the name of science.

As Myrdal promised, then, the concealed *non sequitur* (indeed, the plain nonsense) is readily discovered "when inferences are confronted with premises." It is undeniable that behaviorism has been invaded by "uncontrolled influences from the valuation sphere." The nature of these influences will be explored later.

FOUR

Technology and Others — The Heart of Humanistic Psychology

In the mid-1950s, large numbers of psychologists, particularly clinical and social psychologists, began to revolt against 50 years of reductive behaviorism. They rallied around the banner of Abraham Maslow, the psychologist who spearheaded the attack against the "means-centeredness" and "scientism" of academic behavioristic psychology in America. Traditional psychoanalytic theory, as well as cognitive theories in psychology, was abandoned for the promise held out by existentialism.

The humanist credo was articulated by Maslow (1961) on the occasion of the birth of the *Journal of Humanistic Psychology*:

> The Journal of Humanistic Psychology is being founded by a group of psychologists and professional men and women from other fields who are *interested in those human capacities and potentialities* that have no systematic place either in positivistic or behavioristic theory or in classical psychoanalytic theory, e.g., *creativity, love, self, growth, organism, basic need gratification, self-actualization, higher values, ego-transcendence, objectivity,*

autonomy, identity, responsibility, psychological health, etc.
(p. 1; italics ours)

As Maslow noted, these themes had already made their appearance in the writings of, among others, Goldstein, Fromm, Horney, Rogers, and Allport. But it remained for Maslow to articulate with the strongest voice the concerns of humanistic psychology. Thus, despite the heterogeneity of those who consider themselves "Third Force" psychologists, Maslow has been considered the leading spokesman, the figurehead, if not the founding father.

Thus, the humanistic, or "Third Force" movement in psychology was less a discipline than a protest movement—a protest against the value premises of behaviorism, psychoanalysis, and the conservative world that both were seen to represent. As we noted earlier, most criticisms of and reactions against the behaviorist movement have been in terms of philosophical-religious-political themes rather than in the scientific domain. It is not unusual, then, that the humanistic movement has an antipodal philosophical-religious-political posture. Indeed, the battleground between the two movements is more reminiscent of religious conflict than of scientific-intellectual debate. The war being waged is not one directed toward establishing which movement is more "correct" or "better" but, instead, toward recruiting advocates.

Maslow (1967) has, in fact, been explicit about the religious nature of his Theory of Metamotivation: *"Many of the ultimate religious functions are fulfilled by this theoretical structure."* One of the central concepts of his theory, the B-values (Being-values) are, according to him, worthy of commanding "adoration, reverence, celebration, sacrifice. They are worth living for and dying for."

With this religious fervor as background, it is no surprise that the Association for Humanistic Psychology has produced some of the most militant rhetoric psychology has witnessed. Their battle cry echoes in contrast to the call of the behaviorists—"Down with method and rigor; up with man!" Except for a few attempts, there has been little concern and even less activity among the humanists in the realm of traditional theory formulation and research. Instead, humanistic psychology has somehow evolved into an activity-oriented, group movement that deals almost solely with "nonverbal experience, altered states of consciousness, techniques with which groups and individuals can find new definitions of themselves" (Criswell & Peterson, 1972).

Underlying this activity orientation are value premises, not hidden as Myrdal suggests they might be, but rather proudly expressed as the Humanistic Ethic. Bugental (1971) articulates five tenets to which many Third Force psychologists subscribe:

> The foundation postulation of the humanistic ethic is that each person is the *most responsible agency in his own life* . . . A second tenet . . . is that the ideal relationships between people is one of mutuality between persons each of whom is the subject of his own life and each of whom values and recognizes the subjecthood of the other. This is *Buber's "I-thou" relation* . . . A third tenet . . . may be designated in a shorthand way as the here-and-now perspective. This outlook reminds us that one *always lives only at the present moment* . . . A fourth phase of the humanistic ethic is the recognition that such *emotions* as pain, conflict, grief, anger, and guilt *are parts of the human experience* to be understood and even valued . . . A final aspect . . . has to do with the *seeking for growth-facilitating experiences* which is characteristic of people who have *incorporated the humanistic ethic* (pp. 11–12; italics ours)

The explicit values, as well as the implicit image of man conveyed by the humanists, are clearly reactions against the behaviorists' liquidation of not only mind and experience, but man himself. This attempt to reinstate man, his mind and his experience, into the domain of psychology has been, as we will soon see, transformed into some rather peculiar manifestations with respect to both theory and practice.

Humanistic Jargon

Although Maslow's central ideas and conceptions do not represent all of the Third Force thinking, an exploration of his themes provides more than a little insight into the mainstream of the humanistic movement. Moreover, as Maslow himself suggested, his writings and concepts have indeed commanded the "adoration, reverence, celebration, sacrifice" of numerous psychologists, clergymen, students, and laymen. Thus, Maslow's work has struck a communal chord among the advocates of humanism.

Discontented with the reduction of man to the sum of responses to stimuli, the interrelationships of cognitive symbols, and the subtle interchange between id, ego, and superego, Maslow responded by opening the frontier to the whole of human experience. His forty years of vigorous professional activity were aimed at producing a theory that would enrich the understanding of human experience. Thus, concepts like *peak experiences, Being—and Deficiency—realms, self-actualization, Eupsychia, Theory Z management, high and low grumbles, metaneeds, metamotivations, metahedonism* found their way into the psychological vocabulary.

Although Maslow expressed concern with all levels of human experience, to a large extent he limited his later explorations to the experiences available to self-actualizing individuals. In part, the focus upon the healthy, mature individual was a movement away from the traditional emphasis placed upon the unhealthy, immature individuals studied by the behaviorists and antihumanists.

Maslow's ideas about self-actualizing individuals gave rise to his "Theory of Metamotivation" (1967), which is presented in the format of twenty-eight "testable" propositions. He does not, however, disclose the manner by which these propositions may be tested, nor does he clearly specify the meaning of self-actualization. A brief examination of some of these testable propositions will be sufficient to indicate that Maslow, like Skinner, presents us with nothing more than his own value premises in the guise of a "theory"; that his propositions and central concepts, like Skinner's, are tautological and untestable. Unlike Skinner, however, Maslow expresses a great love of mankind, particularly of individuality and of freedom—yet, as we will see, his work has transformed *most* people into something less than human.

Proposition I—*Self-actualizing individuals* (more matured, *more fully-human*), *by definition*, already suitably gratified in their basic needs, are now motivated in other higher ways, to be called "metamotivations" (italics ours).

Implicit in this initial formulation is that non-self-actualizing individuals, which would include almost everyone, are motivated by base impulses, are less mature, and are not as fully human as the self-actualizers. Thus, the ordinary motives of people below the level of self-actualization are determined by basic needs, while the extraordinary motives of self-actualized people are "metaneeds." This "testable" proposition, then, tells us that to be self-actualizing, *by definition*, a person is "metamotivated." How do we know that he is metamotivated? Because he is self-actualizing. Circularity is by no means the exclusive property of the behaviorists.

The twenty-seven propositions that follow merely compound the intellectual disorder and impoverishment of the first, underlying tenet. Let us sample, therefore, other propositions that Maslow has formulated about the "Supermen" he has chosen to focus his humanism upon.

Proposition II—All such people are devoted to some task, call, vocation, beloved work ("outside themselves").

Proposition V—At this level the dichotomizing of work and play is transcended . . .

Proposition VI—Such vocation-loving individuals tend to identify (introject, incorporate) with their "work" and to make it into a defining characteristic of the self.

Proposition IX—This introjection means that the self has enlarged to include aspects of the world . . . the *distinction between self and not-self* (outside, other) *has been transcended*. (italics ours)

Proposition X—*Less evolved persons* seem to use their work more often for achieving gratification of lower basic needs, of neurotic needs, as a means to an end, out of habit, or as a response to cultural expectations, etc. . . . (italics ours)

Proposition XII—These intrinsic values are instinctoid in nature . . . The "illnesses" resulting from deprivation of intrinsic values (metaneeds) we may call metapathologies . . .

On the basis of this humanistic metatheory, then, a poorly

educated, assembly-line worker who is bored with his job (he is not devoted to some beloved work), who looks forward to weekends when he can go fishing (he dichotomizes work and play), who, nonetheless, works as much overtime as he can in order to earn enough money to send his oldest daughter to college (he works as a means to an end) without sacrificing the care of his other children (he works to achieve gratification of lower, basic needs), suffers from "metapathologies," illnesses resulting from the deprivation of those instinctive "metaneeds." Thus, the "human capacities and potentialities" exhibited by "self-actualizing" individuals, which is the focus of the humanistic psychologists, *by definition*, exclude most of mankind.

Although in closing his essay, Maslow acknowledges his debt to eastern, western, theist, and non-theist religions, one would be hard put to find in those references the source of the disdain implied by humanistic doctrine for man as he struggles to survive, and often strives to do more than that, in an increasingly complex, impersonal world. It seems that disregard for the average man is not the sole property of the behaviorists.

It might be argued that this selective and sparse presentation of humanistic thought has ignored some of the more recent conceptual developments, particularly those that have evolved from encounter groups and other group experience. In fairness, then, let us examine some of the new concepts in humanistic psychology.

In response to charges made by Koch (1969) against some of the manifestations of Third Force psychology, Haigh (1969), at that time president of the Association for Humanistic Psychology, emphasized that the humanistic orientation focuses upon "the experiencing *person*." He elaborated, then, on the consequences of this orientation:

. . . the Association encourages attention to topics having little place in existing systems, such as *love, creativity, spontaneity, play, warmth, ego-transcendence, autonomy, responsibility, authenticity, meaning, transcendental experience, courage.* (p. 4; italics ours)

Haigh's statement is almost identical to the ideas expressed earlier by Maslow (1961). Indeed, as Koch (1971) notes, the language of humanistic psychology, always embedded in statements of intention, represents nothing more than a "swollen word-string . . . of the staple existential 'goodies,' the names of which preempt half the verbal output of the 'humanistic' literature . . ." Even Carl Rogers (1969), from whom one might expect an original comment, describes the "rich, wild, new tapestry that is the intensive group experience" in the same old way: "freedom," "trust," "spontaneous," "flexible," "closer to feelings," "open to experience," "expressively intimate," "I-thou relationships," and so on.

The liturgical form that the humanistic language has taken has a number of ramifications. The indiscriminate repetitive use of words so full of intricate subtleties that philosophers and linguists have for years struggled with their essence, renders these words meaningless, *coarse* representations of "delicately bounded and humanly valuable discriminations" (Koch, 1971). Thus, just as the behaviorists have eliminated the chance for understanding man by using object rather than people language, the humanists have done the same by destroying the meaning of people language. Koch (1971), dismayed by the coarsening and degrading of the usage of words, remarks that one outcome is a loss of actual knowledge:

An individual's conception of the application conditions for a word is a fact of sensibility. Coarsening of language means coarsening of knowledge, and a language community that uses language in a coarsened way is a community of coarsened sensibility. (p. 125)

Just how the sensibility of the humanists has been affected by the destruction of word meanings will be seen in the section concerning their practices. Here, we are concerned with its effect upon the research productions of humanistic psychology.

Maslow (1967) assured us that his theory of metamotivation does have scientific merit and research potential: "[Various experiences] can be assimilated to this theoretical structure and can be tested in an empirically meaningful way, i.e., phrased in a testable way." Despite this assurance, it would indeed be a futile exercise to examine humanistic psychology in terms of its research productions and scientific merit—it simply has none. For some humanistic psychologists this lack is, in fact, a source of pride. For others, especially those who had in the past, made some commitment to the scientific enterprise, this lack is a source of embarrassment. Thus, Rogers (1969), after wholeheartedly endorsing the value of intensive group experience, is able to suspend (if not eliminate) his judgment when summarizing the research productions in this area: "None of the research studies on outcomes of group experience is a masterpiece of precision." Unmindful of the lack of precision, Rogers goes on to report the "research" findings: "*Most* have found *some* changes in self-concept, in attitudes, and in behavior, and a *reasonable* number of these changes persist over time" (italics ours).

Obviously, the language used to express humanistic theory is not intended to "be tested in an empirically meaningful way." Maslow's followers have, in a sense, contradicted him by neglecting entirely the "research potential" of his theory. With disregard and, often, disdain for elementary forms of evidence, the humanistic psychologists pursue "the rich, wild, new tapestry"—the intensive group experience. Thus, it is not hard-won knowledge or insights and understanding to which the humanists have committed themselves, but rather to what Rogers (1969) has described: "milling around," "lashing out," "revealing self," "here-and-now trust," "cracking masks," "feedback," "confrontation," "basic encounter."

Bugental (1971), in his charge to fellow humanists, explains more fully their role:

> If an evolved humanistic ethic is to make its contribution to the evolutionary stream of man's development it will require our courage, our dedication, and our persistence. (p. 24)

Just as the behaviorists have created "the curious presumption that hardly anything new remains to be discovered in a field that has barely been studied" (Asch, 1959), so the humanists have evolved a similar stance. Bugental's call is appropriate for a crusader embarking upon his holy task to convert the infidels—to show them the light. As Bakan (1967) describes it, both the humanists and behaviorists have lost the "sense of search" and have too quickly fixed upon a method, a device, a concept; in short, both groups have become idolaters.

Since the goals of those two groups are different—for the behaviorists, to "dehomunculize" man, and for the humanists to facilitate the transcendence of distinguishing between self and others—the methods also differ. The energies of the humanistic movement have almost exclusively been directed toward developing technologies for group activities. Let us now examine some of those technologies.

Humanistic Technolatry

While the behaviorists have been quietly worshipping the scientific method in their laboratories, the humanists have been engaged in a far more public idolatry of the technology of human growth, self-actualization, and human potential. Divorced from the scientific enterprise and, therefore, freed of the many preoccupations characteristic of research psychologists, the humanists have developed a public-spirit-mindedness. In keeping with this, they have entered the world of business, education, religion, and politics.

A partial compendium of the humanistic technology is provided in Criswell and Peterson's (1972) *Whole Soul Catalog*. The authors warn us that the catalog is not a consumer's guide but rather a report of "the apocalyptic claims of believers." They further caution, "Like merchants at the dawn of the consumer-goods age, the advocates of self-realization now have more enthusiasm than performance record." With this in mind, let us explore some of the marketplace manifestations of humanistic psychology.

ASCID refers to the Altered States of Consciousness Induction Device, designed after a swing purportedly used by medieval witches. The person is immobilized as he is rocked through space, producing "deep trips" and "visions." For those who would prefer a different device, there exist numerous biofeedback machines that allow a person to monitor and possibly control his output of alpha waves—the necessary ingredient of metameditation. For those who prefer not to use gadgets, there is progressive relaxation, autogenic training, the *I Ching*, Zen, witchcraft, chanting, organic food, fasting, and even sensory deprivation to assist the actualization process. Massay, Tai-Chi Chuan, structural integration (Rolfing), all of which involve body manipulation, are available to those who prefer sensual stimulation. The sociable self-actualizer, however, has a multitude of growth and self-expansion opportunities such as marathon sessions, basic encounter groups, gestalt groups, open encounter groups, organizational development groups, theater game and psychodrama groups, *t* (training) groups, women's liberation groups, nude encounter groups, gay liberation groups, Jesus people groups, human potential expander groups, or cojoint family therapy groups. .

To those who might contend that these manifestations of Third Force psychology are a distortion and debasement of Maslow's work, we let Maslow (1967) himself answer:

> In principle, therefore, all the principles and exercises which help to develop (or teach) our sensory awarenesses, our body awarenesses, our sensitivities to the inner signals . . .—all these apply also, though less strongly, to our inner metaneeds . . .
>
> It is this experiential richness which in principle should be "teachable" or recoverable I feel confident, at least in degree, perhaps with the proper use of psychedelic chemicals, with Esalen-type, non-verbal methods, with meditation and contemplation techniques, with further study of the peak experiences, or of B-cognition, etc. (p. 126)

Almost all of the present humanistic psychology movement is given to the pursuit of releasing the growth potential of man. Thus, it is with no small disappointment that some of its sympathizers have viewed the present activities of the Association for Humanistic Psychology. For example, Koch (1969) after wandering into one of their group sessions where "about

70 young humanists, mainly ladies, were lying on the floor in an intertwined and palpating mass" was curious enough to attend a symposium at the American Psychological Association (a few years ago) conducted by a humanist psychologist, Paul Bindrim. Bindrim, the originator of "nude-marathon group therapy," had an overflow audience to whom he explained a therapeutic technique of his own: "crotch-eyeballing." He notes that the crotch is the locale of at least three major hang-ups: (1) aftermath difficulties of toilet training; (2) masturbation guilts; and (3) stresses of adult sexuality. In order to erase all the pathology at one time, "two group members aid in the 'spread-eagling' of a third member" while the rest of the group is told to stare long and hard at the "offending target area." Every member of the group has the opportunity to "benefit from this refreshing psychic boost." Although Bindrim is encouraged by the results, he is waiting until more data are in before giving a decisive assessment.

Bindrim acknowledges his debt to Maslow, who once speculated that in nude groups, "people would go away more spontaneous, less guarded, less defensive, not only about the shape of their behinds, but freer and more innocent about their minds as well."

Koch grants that this is only one of the many approaches employed by humanistic psychologists. Nonetheless, he concludes that "all these methods are based on *one* fundamental assumption: that total psychic transparency—total self-exposure —has therapeutic and growth-releasing potential."

The more obvious and more publicized human crises occasionally precipitated by intensive group experiences such as "psychotic breakdowns," suicides, or divorces (see Shostrom, 1969, "Group Therapy: Let the Buyer Beware"), have overshadowed the more destructive, insidious potential of these groups. By providing, as Koch (1971) notes, "a convenient psychic whorehouse for the purchase of a gamut of well-advertised existential 'goodies': authenticity, freedom, wholeness, flexibility, community, love, joy," encounter-type groups simplify, distort, and coarsen our sensibilities. Manipulative gimmicks, simplistic lexicon, and psychic striptease replace the intelligent, sensitive struggle of man attempting to come to terms with himself, with others, and with the world.

Beneath these methods, devices, and concepts is the ultimate goal of man becoming an undifferentiated, "diffused region in a social space inhabited concurrently by all other men thus diffused." Thus, the behaviorists have completely *emptied* us while the humanists, removing any inner life, have completely *expanded* us.

Rollo May (1972), one of the founders of the Association for Humanistic Psychology, after attending their annual meeting, was prompted to write in a recent Association *Newsletter* that an "aura of irresponsibility . . . ran through the whole program" from the provocative titles of sessions to the wholesale advertising and marketing of encounter groups to the creeping (we think galloping) anti-intellectualism. As Rollo May writes:

> Certainly humanism ought to be a movement toward the total man, which includes feeling, experiencing, deciding, thinking, reflecting, present and historical, etc. Our tendency in our reaction against APA [American Psychological Association] has been an anti-intellectual one and we have tended to leave out the thinking, reflecting, historical man and put in only the feeling, touching man in the "now." This is anti-humanistic.

Thus, more than the work of the behaviorists, even Skinner, the humanistic psychology movement threatens human dignity. Although the behaviorists have denied the existence of an inner life in the name of science, we are allowed still to keep our inner homunculi to ourselves. Humanistic psychology, as Koch (1969) notes, obliterates entirely "the content and boundary of the self by transporting it out of the organism—not merely to its periphery, but right out into public, social space."

This brief discussion of the two major domains of present-day psychology, behaviorism and humanism, leaves us at a grave impasse. It might, of course, be argued that we did not consider numerous psychological theories and that they, perhaps, are more intelligent, more logical, and more fruitful. Admittedly, some theories, concepts, and research strategies exist in psychology that are meaningful and worthwhile. These, however, do not represent the mainstreams of American psychology—but, instead, exist on the periphery or reside in other disciplines altogether. We will, however, turn to some of these alternative perspectives in our final chapter. We have, in addition, omitted many of the clinical or personality theories since they have already been criticized by numerous authors. Here, the purpose was simply to examine the *ideologies* of today's dominant perspectives of American psychology.

Believing Is Seeing or Not Looking—I: Psychological Research

We have witnessed during this century the most enormous social, political, economic, and personal upheavals in recorded history: the economic dislocations of millions of people, the mass executions of political and religious "misfits," the death of millions of soldiers and citizens through war, and the threat of the destruction of humanity. And the leaders of psychology have wrestled with those issues by being preoccupied with the unconscious (Freud), Eastern religion and self-actualization (Maslow), the "dehomunculization" of man (Skinner), the denial of consciousness (Watson), the robotization of man (Hull), and the joy of man (Schutz).

This apparent apathy toward the human situation has not been a function of professional psychologists' malevolence, misanthropy, or willful avoidance—except, perhaps, for the purists attempting to emulate physicists with their laboratories full of glittering gadgets. Indeed, in recent years, most graduate students and many psychologists have expressed concern as well as a commitment to do *something* about the human condition. The major obstacle psychology faces in making a significant contribution in this area has been the inability of psychologists to translate their concern into meaningful, intelligent, professional behavior.

Mainstream psychology, as we have discussed, is far removed from the human situation. Its theories, embedded in the dominant political, economic, and theological ideologies, have led professional psychologists to uphold these ideologies rather than to examine their impact on the lives of others. Thus, psychologists have, with great success, transformed mainstream values and attitudes into absolute "scientific truths," and have provided a spurious technology to interested observers that obscures man's relationship to other men and to society at large. In short, it appears that psychology has offered little to the enterprise of understanding the human condition, and that which it has offered obscures rather than clarifies the problems at hand.

In our earlier chapters, we presented an analysis that attempted to demonstrate that the "scientific method" employed by psychologists was merely a set of ritualized activities based upon behavioristic ideology. It was shown that this "method" could not stand upon its own because of inconsistencies and fallacious logic. In brief, that discussion enabled us to see how beliefs and ideology were transformed into ritual and pseudoscientific "methodology." As a consequence of this ideological transformation, any investigator who utilized this experimental method would obtain "data" that invariably supported the notion that man is a passive recipient of external or internal forces. It is not our purpose, however, to simply demonstrate that conceptual chaos and illogic reign supreme in the psychological enterprise. Instead, beginning with Myrdal's (1967) observation that "Ignorance, like knowledge, is purposefully directed," we will explore the purpose of the vast regions of misinformation in mainstream psychology by examining the relationship between psychological research and its supporting extra-scientific systems.

The Rack as a Paradigm for Psychology

Although many critics of contemporary psychological research complain that scientific psychology emulates the natural sciences (see Bakan, 1967; Bugental, 1963; Koch, 1959; Sanford, 1965), upon closer inspection, we find that the investigatory techniques of psychology resemble, instead, an earlier method of seeking the truth. Specifically, the scientific method as employed by psychological researchers is more akin to the sixteenth-century rack as a method for obtaining the truth than to nineteenth-century physics. We do not, of course, draw any parallel between the inhumanity of this method during medieval times and present psychology; to view the rack simply as a torture device used by malevolent, ignorant people is to misconstrue the meaning of this paradigm. Its use during the Inquisition, for instance, was not merely a function of sadism, but rather reflected the most important religious and political ideology of that time. Indeed, one can readily imagine that many inquisitional examiners were genuinely interested in the saving of souls and in the search for truth.

During this period of history, the nature and order of human relationships were clearly defined by theological practice and political rule. There were those designed to command and others to obey. To attempt to redefine this "natural order of things" was to commit an act of heresy and treason. Within this social context, as an extension of religious and political ideology, it is no surprise to find the rack used as a means of obtaining the truth. The art of gentle persuasion to arrive at the truth would have been in itself an act of heresy—it would have implied that some degree of equality existed in the social order between the inquisitor and those destined to be questioned. The rack was a concrete translation of ideology into ritual—a physical enactment of the belief that there were people destined to power and licensed to search for truth and beauty, and other people destined to be powerless and susceptible to the devil, ugliness, and deceit. Thus, in the "natural" order of things, there were masters and slaves, kings and serfs, God and man, the state and the individual, the church and its flock.

The search for the truth about human conduct was carefully modeled after the ideology and propriety norms supported at the time by church and state. A diagrammatic representation (see Figure 2) of the "proper" relationship between the truth-seeker and the target of his search would depict a vertical arrow of social power drawn from the seeker to the target, exercised in only one direction. The rack as a technology designed to obtain truth, therefore, was primarily a microcosmic construction of the broader social reality. It supported these systems through visual enactment that made the abstract truth of the "good social order" into a concrete and living truth (see Szasz, 1970). In summary, the rack, packaged in ideology, created the impression of an absolute unalterable "reality."

The antithesis of the rack as a technology in the service of truth is the physical experiment or investigation. Since there is no social order, ideology, or propriety norms of social interaction between a person and the inanimate in the physical experiment, we simply have a person observing objects or events. The chemist and physicist do not, in their research,

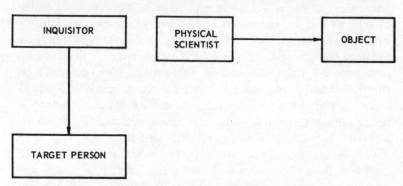

Figure 2.   The rack and physical science paradigms.

have to express loyalty to superiors nor do they have to demonstrate the "reality" of value premises concerning the "natural scheme of things" in the universe. Instead, we have an observer who takes an appreciative stance toward events and objects quite unlike himself or other people. Schematically (again, see Figure 2), we can present this situation as a person connected to an object by a horizontal arrow denoting no interaction but rather a person acting upon an object. The physicist does not interact with but acts upon an object, and then observes the events initiated by the particular form of action in which he engaged. The examiner or inquisitor using the rack paradigm might believe that no interaction has occurred, but rather that he (via the rack) has acted upon the person as if he were an object. Hull, among others, explicitly maintains this idea and encourages other scientists to share this myth.

To "see" people as if they were objects is not enough to make the psychological experiment similar to the settings found in the physical sciences. The use of object language is not enough to transform a person into a thing, except perhaps in the mind of the experimenter. Now, if we compare the experimental paradigm in psychology with both the rack and the physical paradigms, we find that, in many respects, it emulates the rack paradigm while it does not fit the paradigm of the physical sciences.

In the psychological experimental paradigm, we have the same scheme of social order associated with the rack. That is, we have the manipulator and those who are manipulated, the same extreme status differentials, the same single direction of legitimized action, and only the experimenter licensed to construct what is "real" in the situation. There are, of course, some differences between the rack and psychological experiments. These differences, however, can be understood in terms of social power rather than in terms of the scientific enterprise. That is, as the nature of the social order changes, so does the nature of the relationship between the experimenter and the subject.

Today, as in the past, status hierarchies, uneven distribution of social power, and authoritarian organizational structures are still valued and still exist. In theological and political systems, we have lines of command with one person at the top and many at the bottom. Even our economic subsystems exhibit an uneven distribution of wealth and social power. There are employers and the employed; the powerful and the weak. We are not engaging in a dispute as to whether this is "good" or "bad" but instead indicating that it exists today as it has existed for thousands of years. In this sense, the hierarchical order, an important and dominant social motif, can be represented in a vertical schema. The "experimental" paradigm, like the rack in its day, can also be seen as a microcosmic social construction modeled after the vertical social order in the social systems that support the profession.

As we have stated, there are differences between the rack paradigm and the experimental paradigm. Again, these differences are not the outcome of the scientific method, but merely reflect some of the changes that have occurred over time in the political, economic, and theological subsystems in western society. Divine right has given way to legislated right; monarchies to republics. The rise of the power of the citizen is mirrored in our truth-seeking paradigms (although this was not true in Nazi Germany) by the use only of volunteer subjects. That is, the volunteer gives the experimenter the right or power to manipulate. It is not surprising, then, to find that as our society is enmeshed in a controversy concerning civil rights and liberties, we find a corresponding controversy within the psychological profession over the rights of subjects in experiments (see Kelman, 1968; Smith, 1969).

Thus, the vertical social arrangement of the Middle Ages has, to some extent, given way to a more horizontal one. Although the experimental paradigm is an analogue of a more liberal, egalitarian social arrangement, psychologists, nonetheless, act as if they had full reign over the experimental situation. Once the volunteer becomes a subject, he is no longer seen or treated as a person, let alone a peer. At the inception of the investigation the social power is transferred to the experimenter, and it is only his perspective that becomes the basis of "true-unalterable reality." The conception of man that the experimenter supports, and the ideologies he translates into concrete rituals, remain similar to those that existed centuries ago.

To contrive experiments, to manipulate variables, to keep subjects naïve, to ignore and deny the subject's experience, and to retranslate ideology into correlation coefficients or main effects on an analysis of variance table, is to engage in complex activities designed to convince an audience (and often oneself) of the truth of one's beliefs. God's will, rather than man's, defines theological doctrine; the state, rather than the individual, defines political doctrine; the corporation, rather than the individual, defines economic doctrine; and the psychological experiment, rather than human experience, defines psychological theory and research.

Risks of the Rack

The users of the rack must have, at times, met some recalcitrant subjects who offered "data" that threatened the inquisitioners' conception of the "truth." Moreover, we are certain that they were able to assimilate the disconfirming information in such a manner that it was ultimately transformed into evidence that supported their beliefs. We know this because, centuries later, highly trained, scientific observers confronted with "bad" subjects who elicit "wrong" responses have dealt with these "data" in a medieval, sophistic fashion. For example, in a study of role taking conducted by Helfand (1956), it was predicted that schizophrenics would show poorer role-taking abilities than nonschizophrenics. That is, they would be unable to identify with others; to "get into their shoes." To Helfand's surprise, however, the differences he found favored his schizophrenic subjects. Helfand interpreted these findings as follows:

> What is it that permits, or enables the schizophrenic to respond with such sensitivity? Secondly, why do they respond with such sensitivity? . . . The behavior of the normal individual was to project a preconceived set of ideas based primarily on a com-

monly shared cultural stereotype (in the experimental situation). The patients, responding to the same information, made better use of it, although their reactions were highly idiosyncratic. Sarbin's description of the schizophrenic as *lacking a "generalized other"* concept seems appropriate to the results here. The schizophrenic, possibly because of this lack, responded to the cues as he perceived them. . . . The schizophrenics' . . . *lack of a conventional frame of reference* . . . served to contribute to their hyperacuity . . . assuming that schizophrenics lack this generalized other, such an *impairment with resultant hyperacuity,* should be found in younger children, and in emotionally disturbed children as compared to well-adjusted children of the same age. (pp. 39–40; italics ours)

In Helfand's interpretation, the unpredicted superiority of the schizophrenic subjects in role-taking skills is "explained" as a result of a putative lack of a "generalized other." Seen now as a consequence of a psychological *deficit,* the schizophrenics' skills are transformed into a liability, and Helfand can conclude by comparing his subjects to emotionally disturbed children. His belief concerning the deficiencies of schizophrenics remains intact. He has merely added a new defect to the long list attributed to schizophrenia.

Similarly, Richman, Kellner, and Allen (1968), confronted with the unanticipated and embarrassing findings that organic retardates were more accurate than familial retardates, who in turn were more accurate than normals in their judgments of size constancy, try to salvage their theory in the following manner:

The findings of greater size constancy among organics than among familial retardates or normal adolescents is somewhat surprising. It is possible that the superior veridicality of the brain-injured Ss in this investigation may be partly explained in terms of Werner's (1948) concept of "developmental arrest" . . . It is clear that organic retardates (and to a lesser extent familial retardates) exhibit a relative lack of conceptual functioning and thus remain somewhat fixated at the sensory-motor and/or perceptual level of cognitive development. It is also conceivable, however, that within these more *"primitive" areas of intellectual functioning*, and in particular, the area of perceptual-motor operations . . . that a *lack of subordination to higher level, conceptual operations* is accompanied by a greater differentiation and refinement of available perceptual response patterns in organic retardates. (pp. 581–582; italics ours)

According to this interpretation, the unexpected superiority in performance of the organic and familiar retardates was the result of a putative lack of a higher-order conceptual system. Accuracy in size perception, previously regarded as a psychological asset, is now seen as a consequence of a psychological deficit. To uphold the authors' beliefs concerning mental retardates, they must transform the retardate's *ability* into a *liability*.

The infinite latitude for the interpretation of data that is available to the psychologist draws the rack-as-paradigm even closer to the psychological enterprise. Both the inquisitor and the researcher have been mandated to define reality; yet, neither one is bound to the constraints imposed by their subjects' experience or behavior. It is their own ultimate judgment based upon their preconceptions that takes precedence over any observation. The inquisitor was guaranteed success in obtaining the "reality" he expected and desired by the amount of physical force he could exert on the subject. The psychological researcher is also guaranteed success in meeting his expectations by the amount of ambiguity he can generate in the experimental situation. Force and ambiguity have the same consequences when seeking the truth; both not only allow but encourage the seeker to verify his expectations.

Another parallel that can be drawn between the rack and the experiment concerns the subjects. The most common recipients of the rack were the unfortunates of society. That is, people who were "suspect" because of either religious, political, or social deviancy. When the research technology of psychology is applied to the marketplace (outside the walls of the university), we find that it is again the unfortunates of society who are the recipients. It is both interesting and informative to examine where psychologists have and have not searched for the "truth" and with whom they have conducted their search.

Believing Is Not Looking

Nowhere can the handmaiden functions of psychology be seen more clearly than at the profession's interface with the people of a culture. That is, once we examine who are studied and treated by the profession—and how they are studied and treated—the handmaiden functions become clear. It is at the public interface that psychology comes under the close scrutiny of those agencies that support it. It is here that psychology must demonstrate its allegiance to the economic, political, and theological values of society. In this section, then, we will examine what transpires between psychology and the marketplace by examining who are the subjects of psychological research. Knowledge of a profession's target populations offers insight into what is approved and disapproved of by mainstream society. In this sense, this may lead to the understanding of the social taboos of a particular culture, and whether the profession responds to these taboos. If our thesis is correct, that is, if psychology is "politically conditioned" to be nothing more than what society wants it to be, we would expect the following:

(a) psychologists avoid studying those who support the profession and the systems to which they belong (e.g., political, religious, economic leaders);

(b) psychologists avoid studying any aspect of the human situation that can embarrass the people and the systems that support them;

(c) psychologists, when they do engage in research in the marketplace, apologize for mainstream society.

Since most of the financial and legal support for the psychological profession (and here we include clinical as well as research activities) comes from governmental agencies, we would expect that political leaders would escape the scrutiny of the psychologist. Except for rare occasions, the examination of political officials appears to be taboo. The behavior of psychologists at such times is best illustrated by their response to the candidacy of Barry Goldwater for President. Senator

Goldwater's outspoken dislike for and distrust of social scientists (particularly psychologists) no doubt helped justify their diagnosis of him as being "psychologically unfit."

From a traditional empirical perspective, however, psychological intrusion into the sphere of political leadership is all but nonexistent. In a personal communication, Greenstein, a political scientist, noted that in the past 72 years, only six empirical studies that dealt directly with personality characteristics of government officials have been accomplished. Four of the six studies were conducted by nonpsychologists. Although the value of such research is obvious, Greenstein (1969) observes that:

> The study of personality and politics is, in fact, not a thriving scholarly endeavor. A principal reason is that the scholars who study politics do not feel equipped to analyze personality in ways that meet their intellectual standards . . . If the political scientist persists in his determination to make systematic use of psychology, he is likely to experience further discouragement. Much of the research and theory he will encounter will seem singularly irrelevant to explaining the kind of complex behavior that interests him. And where psychological writers *do* address themselves to this subject matter, their political observations will often seem naive and uninformed. Psychologists' insights seem irrelevant to political scientists for the good reason that many psychologists do not conceive of their science as one which *should* attempt to explain concrete instances of social behavior . . . Thus a deliberate attempt is made, as one psychologist puts it, to treat psychology as "socially indifferent"—to strip away and ignore those aspects of behavior that are specific consequences of the fact that it has occurred, say, on a congressional committee or at a political party convention. (p. 13)

Some psychologists have attempted to engage in political research. But, as we noted earlier in this chapter, most psychologists seem to have difficulty applying their concern with real problems and issues into meaningful, intelligent research. However, this is not to say that some of the studies conducted in this area have not been valuable. For instance, psychologists who have examined by means of content analyses the productions of political leaders (speeches, letters, and diaries) have added a great deal of insight and information to our knowledge of public figures. This information, however, generally comes long after the person's years in office are over. Moreover, a number of excellent investigations have been conducted on the voting behavior and political attitudes of the general public.

The approaches utilized by psychologists, in addition to the time of their studies, do not have the same potential for yielding significant information as those approaches they have ignored. The scrutiny of contemporary political figures remains, then, in the domain of journalism.

For the psychologist to redefine his professional goals and beliefs so that political phenomena become a central focus would be to behave as the proverbial dog who bites the hand that feeds it. Judging from the current difficulties journalists are facing, one might argue that avoidance of political topics is a sign of the prudence of psychologists. But as Greenstein (1969) notes, such practical behavior may, in the long run, be very costly:

> The small population of students of personality and politics has as yet not contributed enough that is well established on the impact of personality on politics—much less on the impact of politics on personality . . . It may be that we can limp along for further millennia without clarifying our assumptions about personality and politics and without devoting major intellectual resources to testing the assumptions against reality; but the possible consequences of continuing to muddle through may be too grim to contemplate . . . Even if the probability were slight that psychological inquiry into politics might encourage governing practices that were more firmly located in the world of reality, the risks would seem to warrant more substantial colonies of investigators on the borders between psychology, including personality psychology, and political science. (pp. 152–153)

Despite the small amount of research conducted about political figures, they have, at least, received some attention from psychologists. If we turn, however, to the areas of religion and economics, we find that those leaders have entirely escaped psychological inquiry. Surely, these persons have an cnormous impact on the lives of others, making them worthy subjects for empirical observations. Yet, not one study conducted by psychologists can be found in the literature concerning boards of directors of a large industries, presidents or other executives of large corporations, members of the New York Stock Exchange, or other eminent figures in the world of finance.

Nonetheless, psychologists have been engaged as employees or consultants by these persons to conduct research in corporate settings, even, at times, with top-level management as subjects. This research, however, has been for in-house purposes: for the use of the corporation in order to help it improve organizational functions. It is not, therefore, available to public scrutiny. Psychological literature does abound, however, with extensive research reports concerning lower-level employees (e.g., production line workers), especially in terms of information designed to increase their morale, their attendance, and, in general, their productivity. This, however, is an entirely different matter. It does illustrate, nonetheless, the point we are making: psychologists, when engaged in applied research, do not focus upon the powerful.

Religious leaders, as well as religious organizations, have also been neglected from any empirical studies by psychologists. With the exception of a few fringe religious sects or "far-out" leaders, religion as an area of investigation has been ignored. Yet, psychologists have served the religious enterprise by counseling and providing other therapeutic opportunities to members of the church staff (ministers, priests, rabbis), and by developing the field of "pastoral counseling" to assist pastors in dealing more effectively with the problems of their congregation. These functions are quite different, however, from the research enterprise with which we are concerned.

In short, the empirical intrusion of professional psychologists in the political, economic, and religious spheres is limited. The limitations have not been imposed by scientific considerations but, instead, by extrascientific concerns. More specifically, psychologists study by invitation those areas chosen by the people they serve. Thus, as political, religious, and economic policies have become more progressive, Moynihan (1970) notes that:

Social science was asked, for example, to attest to the equality
of the races; to legitimize the demand of wage workers under
capitalism to organize and bargain collectively; to provide measures of intellectual worth so that applications for college admission and such might be judged by objective criteria; to prescribe
measures for a high-level functioning of the economy. All these
it did. (p. 37)

And that, of course, is exactly the point; psychology has
not only studied issues and problems requested (which in itself,
as Myrdal [1969] notes, may be socially responsive and responsible), but it has generally produced results that are consistent
with the ideologies of those who requested the "scientific"
research. Here, we refer only to "relevant" or applied research.
For the most part, a silent majority of research psychologists
searches for topics to investigate that are relevant only to a hand-
ful of colleagues.

Although the demand for "relevant" research has become
more widespread and more intense in recent years, psychology
has not made any headway into relevant problem areas. In a
personal communication from the editor of one of the leading
APA journals, he remarked that despite the liberalism of most
clinical and social psychologists (and the radicalism of some)
he did not receive a single manuscript concerning the relationship between any psychological variable and the conflict in
Indochina. Indeed, the desire for relevance seems to reflect
the most recent of the fashionably oppressed groups. For
instance, the concern with the oppressed Negro minority, which
led to volumes of research during the 1950s, was overshadowed
during the 1960s with the discovery of the poor (including
whites) on whose condition a war was being waged; more
recently, psychologists' attention has turned again, this time
leading to a proliferation of literature concerning women and
their liberation. It would appear that psychology is fulfilling
its duty with respect to the public welfare and its commitment
to alleviate suffering. An interesting sequence should, however,
be noted; psychological research follows on the heels of oppressed groups becoming "legitimate." Evidence of the legiti-

macy of these groups' right to be studied usually comes in the form of financial assistance from governmental agencies.

This sequence of events does not, of course, make the research in and of itself any less relevant, important, or meaningful. It does, however, indicate the "political conditioning" (Myrdal, 1969) of psychological research and alerts us to the potential consequences of this lack of investigatory autonomy. More specifically, because of their collective caution, psychological researchers have entirely ignored many problem areas, oppressed groups, and social systems that might embarrass (i.e., they are not legitimate) those who support psychology.

Bakan (1971), in his exploration of cruelty, specifically infanticide, comments on just this state of affairs:

> It seems as though we are unable to face not only the problem of child abuse, but the topic of cruelty in general. Cruelty is rarely dealt with in nonfiction . . . I have not been able to find *cruelty* in the library card catalogues as a subject heading. In the Encyclopaedia Britannica, I find only two entries under the word *cruelty* in the index. One of these is *Cruelty* (divorce) and the other *Cruelty to Animal acts*. The failure to list cruelty among common bibliographic subject indices speaks loudly in its silence . . . There is unfortunately a close relationship between the characteristic abhorrence that we have toward the abuse of children and the relative absence of research on the question. It is a most remarkable fact that abundant research material on problems of substantially lesser significance exists; but only very recently has scientific entertainment of the problem of child abuse even entered the realm of possibility. Elizabeth Elmer, in commenting on the scantiness of research on the topic, rightly suggests, I believe, that it can be explained by the taboo . . . regarding abuse and gross neglect (pp. 7–8).

Cruelty and child abuse, critical aspects of the political, economic, religious, and moral values of man, are just two examples of socially unacceptable topics for mainstream psychology. Here we find psychologists responding in the same manner as the general populace with respect to an unsanctioned area. But this is not new to the psychological enterprise.

Psychological research has had a long history of failing

to become entangled in aspects of the human situation that might potentially benefit many people, but might at the same time disconcert certain elitist groups. One of the earliest illustrations of psychological caution involved the political, social, and personal upheavals present at the turn of the century. In a senate committee established to ascertain the relations between labor and capital in 1883, a witness described the social conditions in a large urban area:

> Perhaps next to liquor drinking, the worst ill that afflicts the teenage-wage classes is wretched domiciles—overcrowded, badly ventilated, poisoned by sewer-gas and excessively rented. Thousands of such structures in this [New York] and other large cities, including Chicago, where I reside, should be demolished by municipal authority as nuisances, injurious to the public health. It is a dreadful fact that in this naturally salubrious city the annual mortality exceeds the birth by upwards of ten thousand, as shown by the sanitary statistics of the municipality, proving that were it not for the inflowing stream, the population of New York would become extinct and the city uninhabited . . . (p. 74)

During this period in history there was a wealth of data available to research psychologists, data that had the potential for allowing the profession to construct theories about people and their concerns, as well as models of the social structure in which they lived. An examination of the literature in psychology, its published studies and theoretical works at the turn of the century discloses that psychologists, instead, were preoccupied with introspection, reaction time, perception, learning, and the denial of consciousness. Were we to attempt to construct a picture of the human situation at that time on the basis of the concerns of mainstream American psychology, we would evolve a rather distorted and peculiar portrait, indeed. Our conclusion would have to be that the only problems that confronted psychology and that remained to be answered were those concerning memory, perception, and physiological processes.

After reviewing the state of psychology in 1890, William James, one of its founders, was moved to comment: "It would be difficult to believe that intelligent men could be so guilty of so patent a fallacy, were not the history of psychology there to give proof" (in Jordan, 1968). His remark would still be an appropriate evaluation of the state of psychology.

True to the tradition set forth by the founding fathers of psychology nearly 100 years ago, psychologists still fail to deal with current problems (except, of course, when invited) in a meaningful fashion. A content analysis of psychological publications from 1885 through 1971, with specific emphasis on the years preceding, during, and following significant human events (e.g., World War I, the Great Depression, World War II, ghetto riots, Vietnam War), indicates that almost no studies were conducted that explored the meaning of those events on people. Today's literature of psychology still presents as distorted a picture of the human condition as that reflected by the psychology of the late nineteenth century.

Thus, the value premises of the first psychologists, who represented an elite group of academicians, have been the legacy passed on through graduate training to today's professional psychologists. Despite the controversy over the virtues and vices of "relevant" or "action" research, most psychologists, having incorporated and absorbed these values, remain detached from the debate, certain that "pure" research alone is the path to scientific knowledge.

There have been, nevertheless, occasional studies done outside the laboratory, which have yielded information that might have been potentially useful with respect to man's relationship to society. These studies have met with particularly interesting fates. For instance, in the 1920s, Hartshorne and May were commissioned by a religious organization to conduct a systematic program of research on deceit in children. The organization requested this information so that it might more effectively influence the moral development of children. Hartshorne and May (1928) produced two huge volumes of extensive research that had many moral implications that might have aroused the psychological community to probe further into this area of human conduct. Instead, the work was greeted by research psychologists with methodological criticisms and procedural complaints, completely ignoring the potential it represented in terms of understanding a complex, intriguing human phenomenon. It took nearly forty years for psychologists to reopen their study of deceit and morality in children (Braginsky, 1970).

The landmark study, *The Authoritarian Personality* (Adorno, Frenkel-Brunswik, Levinson & Sanford, 1950), conducted shortly after World War II, focused on the question of the potential for a fascistic movement in this country. It is noteworthy that this research was funded by the Anti-Defamation League of the B'nai B'rith. The publication of this study generated a great deal of controversy (especially concerning methodology), as well as interest, reflected by the sizable number of doctoral dissertations employing the *F*-Scale (Fascism). The majority of the studies, both pre- and postdoctoral, however, simply used one or two attitude scales as independent variables in an investigation of the construct validity of the scales. The emphasis shifted, then, from a focus upon the moral and political implications of authoritarianism to issues such as: high scorers on the authoritarian scale should be better marksmen than low scorers.

The conceptual directions this study plotted, and the questions it raised concerning the role of the family, morality, politics, religion, and personality in the affairs of people were never taken up. Eventually, the popular use of the *F*-scale as an independent variable in research waned, and now it is part of the history of psychology.

Similar sporadic activity has been initiated by other meaningful studies, particularly in the area of social psychology. More often than not, the activity is merely an exercise to fulfill the requirements for a Ph.D. or a journal publication. Fortunately, there are exceptions (these will be discussed in the final chapter) but they are just that—exceptions, not representative of the research productions of mainstream psychology.

Whom and What Psychologists Study

We now know what regions of the human situation psychologists do not empirically research and whom they do not use as subjects for scientific inquiries. Whom and what, then, do they study? When they are not employing as subjects rats, cats, pigeons, worms, monkeys, or fish, research psychologists use college students. Almost 80 percent of the studies conducted on people involve college students, often students who are required to "volunteer" as subjects for psychological experiments as part of their course work. The remainder of subjects is comprised of hospitalized mental patients, institutionalized mental retardates, schoolchildren, youngsters in reformatories, men in prison, and other institutionalized, "captive" groups.

This does not imply that the subjects do not volunteer or that their civil rights and privacy are not respected. Most researchers who employ human subjects in their studies are both sensitive and responsive to these issues. The groups who might frequently participate in psychological research, however, are unrepresentative of mainstream American citizens and, often, are deviant within their own subculture group (surplus populations). Even with respect to sex, the subjects of psychological studies do not approach a representative sampling (51 percent of the population are women, while a much smaller percentage are research subjects), with a preponderance of studies employing males. This is a remarkable oversight, since among all social scientists, psychologists are most aware of sex differences in terms of nearly every psychological dimension ever investigated.

At times, however, psychologists are invited by various societal organizations to examine mainstream populations. For example, during the two world wars, psychologists were needed to develop testing procedures for the sorting and managing of large, heterogeneous groups of men. After these wars (especially World War II), problems associated with stress became increasingly obvious. Thus, with financial support from the government, large numbers of psychologists were recruited and trained to diagnose (sort) and to service the emotionally distressed. We have already noted the voluminous research, again supported by the government, concerning minority groups. Industrial and religious organizations have also made use of the scientific expertise of research psychologists in response to problems directly concerning their organizations. Thus, *what* psychologists investigate and the content areas of their research is determined (directly or indirectly) by the social systems in which they operate.

By now it may appear as though there are large numbers of psychologists engaged in applied research. This, however, is not accurate. In a recent survey of 11,000 psychologists (see *APA Monitor*) only 300 reported that they conducted research in applied areas. There may, of course, be many more psychologists who are doing applied research, but who choose to view their work in a more abstract, theoretical fashion. Since all of the psychologists surveyed are products of similar graduate programs, the ideal research posture is that of the "purist." The term "applied" for most of them is somewhat tainted, particularly when associated with clinical, counseling, or industrial practice (as opposed to research). These value premises have led to schisms within the profession, to the emergence of splinter groups, to new APA divisions, and to new journals.

Thus, psychologists are faced with numerous obstacles when they attempt to make a contribution that is meaningful and relevant to the human condition. First, they may study only what they are invited to study. Second, their training in a scientific method with behavioristic emphasis leaves no room for discovery. And finally, they must be willing to be stigmatized by the academic psychology establishment for working in "applied" areas. We are not trying to romanticize the plight of the "applied" psychologist, whether he is a researcher or a practitioner, but to merely enumerate the societal and professional pressures that exist. Because of these pressures (in addition to others we will discuss shortly), applied psychologists are the apologists for mainstream society and carry with them the morality and values of the systems that support the psychological enterprise.

In their capacity as professionals, applied psychologists do the work frowned upon by purist and academic psychologists, and that paves the way for the irrelevant, "hard-nosed," scientific psychology. Yet, in order to function effectively in their professional tasks, the applied psychologist needs the cloak of scientific respectability (the jargon, the laboratories, the "scientific" findings) provided by the purists.

Thus, in spite of schisms and insulting rhetoric, both groups of psychologists enjoy a perfect symbiotic union. The consequences of this union with respect to psychological practices will be examined next.

SIX

Believing Is Seeing or Not Looking–II: Psychological Diagnosis

We have found that psychologists, for a host of reasons, have avoided the investigation of socially, politically, and morally unsanctioned topics, despite the significance they may have in terms of human welfare and scientific knowledge. In addition, we have noticed that psychologists have neglected to study the elite of society for a number of obvious reasons. What is less obvious, however, is why psychologists expend so much time and effort on the marginal members of society when investigating members of the social structure. The handmaiden functions of the psychological enterprise, only hinted at in the preceding chapter, provide an explanation of why psychology focuses on this deviant segment of the social strata.

Throughout history, every culture has in some way had to cope with the problem of deviancy. For a society to maintain social order, especially with respect to balance, control, and power, it was crucial to identify, to label, and to somehow "treat" its deviant citizens (see Foucault, 1965). The "treatment," on some occasions, took .the form of final solutions by eliminating the social deviants, while, at other times, it emerged in more humane forms. This treatment will be the focus of the next chapter. Here, we will be concerned with the identification and classification of deviants.

Until recently, the church commanded a central role in the maintenance of order, balance, and power within society. Szasz (1970), in a historical account of the church's relationship to deviants in the Middle Ages, comments:

> . . . society was dominated by the Church. In a religious society, deviance is conceptualized in theological terms: the deviant is the witch, the agent of Satan. Thus the sorceress who healed, the heretic who thought for himself, the fornicator who lusted too much, and the Jew who, in the midst of a Christian society, stubbornly rejected the divinity of Jesus—however much they differed from one another—all were categorized as "heretics" and thus was each an enemy of God, persecuted by the Inquisition. The medieval historian, Walter Ullman, put it this way: "Publicly to hold opinions which ran counter to or attacked the faith determined and fixed by law was heresy and the real reason for making heresy a crime was . . . that the heretic showed intellectual arrogance by preferring his own opinions to those that were specially qualified to pronounce upon matters of faith". . .
> (p. 4)

Thus, in order to be classified as a deviant in Medieval Europe, a person had only to publicly disagree with the mainstream value premises embodied in the church. Although the content of the disagreement might widely vary, the label "heretic" was applied to all deviants. Even though the labels now applied are more numerous and sound scientific, today's criteria for classifying deviance is not very different from the medieval criteria. Erikson (1962) notes that "deviance is not a property inherent in certain forms of behavior, it is a property conferred upon these forms by the audiences which directly or indirectly witness them." Similarly, Kitsuse (1962) observes that "it is the responses of the conventional and conforming members of the society who identify and interpret behavior as deviant . . ." Indeed the social interactionist "school" of sociology recognizes that deviancy is in the eye of the beholder and that "the deviant is one to whom the label has been successfully applied" (Becker, 1963).

Centuries ago, the audiences (the conforming members of society who proclaimed what is deviant) were the inquisitors of the church. As we noted in a previous chapter, the functions of the church have largely been taken over by psychology and its medical counterpart, psychiatry. Today, society relies upon these new "high priests" to determine what is deviant, to identify and classify those who are deviant, and to "treat" the deviants. Although their decisions are stated in "scientific" terminology and based upon "scientific" research, the religious value premises underlying this enterprise in our society have been traced to the Protestant Ethic. Beneath the multitude of sophisticated labels lies the dualistic conception of man firmly rooted in the doctrine of predestination—the healthy "elect" and the sick, unchangeable, "damned" (Rotenberg, 1972).

The shift of responsibility from the church to psychology and psychiatry is described by Szasz (1970):

> In the new-secular and "scientific" cultural climate—as in any other—there were still the disadvantaged, the disaffected, and the men who thought and criticized too much. The non-conformist, the objector, in short, all who denied or refused to affirm society's dominant values, were still the enemies of society. To be sure, the proper ordering of this new society was no longer conceptualized as Divine Grace; instead, it was viewed in terms of Public Health. Its internal enemies were thus seen as mad; and Institutional Psychiatry came into being, as had the Inquisition earlier, to protect the group from this threat . . . The original Seventeenth Century definition of madness . . . conformed to the requirements for which it was fashioned. To be considered mad, it was enough to be abandoned, destitute, poor, unwanted by parents or society. (p. 13)

Culture-bound by the dominance of the Protestant Ethic and "politically conditioned" by a capitalistic economic system, it is no surprise, then, that psychologists have focused their attention (research, diagnoses, treatment) on the destitute, the poor, and the unwanted. In recent years, several authors have analyzed the relationship between psychology, psychiatry, and mainstream values (see Haley, 1969; Laing, 1967; Leifer, 1969;

Sarbin, 1967; Szasz, 1961), exploring especially the "correctional stance" (Matza, 1970) toward "misfits." Specifically, unproductive members of society are perceived as unquestionably having intrapsychic problems associated with their surplus status. To be a misfit is to almost automatically be suspect of abnormal psychological functioning. Thus, with their suspicions aroused, psychologists have formulated research hypotheses in order to "scientifically" understand the nature of deviants and to "scientifically" correct their behavior.

Who Are the Misfits?

One of the first "applied" psychological inquiries was conducted at the invitation of the French government in 1904. Alfred Binet, a psychologist, was asked to devise a test to detect children who were too feebleminded and to dull to benefit from ordinary schooling. The scale Binet developed with the assistance of Theodore Simon was published in 1905. This test is the prototype of, by now, scores of contemporary intelligence tests. Although the initial purpose of constructing such instruments has been lost sight of in the burgeoning subscience of psychometric testing, the contemporary measures of intelligence are often used as originally intended. That is, they are used to identify the youngsters who are intellectually deficient and who could not, therefore, benefit from standard educational procedures.

Apart from the often articulated altruistic motives ascribed to the diagnostic enterprise of identifying intellectual misfits (e.g., to provide specialized educational training programs), another reason for their identification is explicit in Fernald's (1912) description of them:

> . . . [the] feebleminded are a parasitic, predatory class never capable of self-support or of managing their own affairs. The great majority ultimately become public charges in some form. They cause unutterable sorrow at home and are a menace and danger to the community. Feebleminded women are almost invariably immoral. We have only begun to understand the

importance of feeblemindedness as a factor in the causation of pauperism, crime and other social problems . . . Every feeble-minded person, especially the high-grade imbecile, is a potential criminal, needing only the proper environment and opportunity for the development and expression of his criminal tendencies. The unrecognized imbecile is a most dangerous element in the community. (pp. 90–91)

The mainstream ideology and value premises so explicit in Fernald's statement are even apparent in the jargon of later scientific description. For instance, Heber (1962), in depicting the typical behavior associated with mental retardation, states that "mental retardates" exhibit:

. . . behavior which does not meet the standards of dependability, reliability, and trustworthiness; behavior which is persistently asocial, anti-social, and/or excessively hostile . . . inability to recognize the needs of other persons in interpersonal interactions . . . inability to delay gratification of needs and lack of long-range goal striving or persistence with response only to short-term goals. (p. 77)

In short, they are the same menacing deviants Fernald described. These youngsters, however, are not the only menaces to the social order. Their more elderly counterparts can be found among the mentally ill, particularly among those labeled schizophrenics. As Schooler and Parkel (1966) warn: "the chronic schizophrenic is not Seneca's 'reasoning animal' or Spinoza's 'social animal,' or even a reasonably efficient version of Cassirer's symbol-using animal." There is, indeed, a striking similarity between Heber's mental retardate and Redlich and Freedman's (1966) schizophrenic:

As the patient becomes deficient in discriminating his outer and inner realities, punitive, infantile, sexual, aggressive, and passive wishes, as well as fantasies and drives, gain prominence, surface to consciousness, and often appear uncontrolled. (p. 464)

The similarity between these two putative defects has led us in an earlier work (Braginsky & Braginsky, 1971) to dub them the Siamese twins of the psychological world. A new sibling, however, has been added to this family of social misfits, one which encompasses a far greater number of people than mental retardation and schizophrenia: namely, the poor. We have already noted that psychologists have been invited to investigate this group; rising to the challenge, they have produced volumes of research.

Miller, Riessman and Seagull (1968), in reviewing the literature on the poor, catalog the behaviors that psychologists have observed:

> . . . relative readiness to engage in physical violence, free sexual expression (as through intercourse), minimum pursuit of education, low aspiration level, failure of parents to identify the class of their children's playmates, free spending, little emphasis on being well-mannered and obedient, and short-time dependence of parents. On the other hand, middle-class persons feel that they *should* save, postpone and renounce a variety of gratifications . . . (p. 416)

The behavior of the lower class, thus, is characterized by an inability to defer gratification, which implies that the poor are incapable of managing their own affairs and unable to control their own impulses. This theme (Deferred Gratification Pattern) appears so frequently in discussions of the lower class that Miller, Riessman, and Seagull (1968) conclude that for many researchers it is "an explanation of why the poor are poor."

Members of the middle class, the mainstream of society, are able to defer impulse gratification through the strategy of "impulse renunciation," while the poor, unable to do so, are "impulse followers." The defect, then, of the lower class is simply a failure to incorporate the Protestant Ethic. However, since they are not only marginal with respect to mainstream society but often dwell within their own "culture of poverty," psychologists perceive the poor as being defective and, therefore, label them deviants.

By now, most objectivity attributed to the psychological research enterprise should be dismissed. Psychologists, when they observe the poor in their own community, see no differently than any other well-integrated member of mainstream society. Rather than openness, fairmindedness, or wisdom, they bring with them the stereotype of the poor that has been with us since the Industrial Revolution. Their observations, therefore, are little more than translations into psychological jargon of the value judgments held by most people who occupy positions of social power.

Psychology seems to have uncovered society's deviants: the stupid, the mad, and the poor. Psychology's contribution to this problem has been to transform stereotypical thinking into clinical descriptions that serve as the basis for "diagnoses," in addition to supplying an array of tests to provide a fuller clinical picture.

Psychodiagnosing the "Misfits"

The single most important distinction between clinical psychologists and psychiatrists, besides a medical degree, is psychological diagnostic testing. Psychiatrists often call upon psychologists to do a psychological "work-up" of a client or patient, to administer and score psychological tests, and to thereby provide an empirical assessment of the client's mental functioning and capacities. How well these tests work, however, has been the subject of controversy since their appearance on the psychological scene.

The shortcomings of tests of intelligence or any human aptitude tests are succinctly described by Sarason and Doris (1969):

> The assessment of intellectual functioning can be made only through tests or procedures that reflect a comprehensive theory of intelligence—a condition not met by the most frequently used tests today. . . . It cannot be too strongly stated that *most of our tests are woefully inadequate for the evaluation of various human aptitudes.* (p. 50; italics ours)

Personality tests (measures of psychodynamic functioning,

conflicts, and drives) do not fare any better than aptitude tests. The two most widely used psychological tests, the Rorschach inkblot test and the Draw-a-Person test (both projective tests), have also been widely researched. Based on their extensive review of the literature, as well as their own research on these tests, Chapman and Chapman (1967, 1969, 1971) suggest that, "In interpreting the results of these tests, the average clinician may project his own preconceptions and assumptions into his description of the patient." Our earlier discussion of the problems presented by studying ambiguous behavior is relevant here, since the data of the clinical psychologist using projective tests are ambiguous, verbal responses to ambiguous, visual stimuli (Rorschach) or merely ambiguous drawings of a person (DAP).

Scores of studies have been done refuting both the reliability and validity of psychodiagnostic tests; nonetheless, many clinical psychologists still use them. Chapman and Chapman (1971) corroborate this observation, particularly with respect to the Draw-a-Person test:

> Most clinicians know about the research showing that the DAP signs are invalid, yet many thousands continue to use the test regularly because they claim *they have seen the signs* work in their own clinical practice. *"I'll trust my own senses* before I trust some journal article," said one clinical psychologist. "I know that paranoids don't seem to draw big eyes in the research labs," said another, "but they sure do in my office." (p. 20; italics ours)

Similarly, it is by now a well-known finding that there is a cultural bias in IQ tests that favors middle-class white persons. Nonetheless, psychologists administer these biased tests of intelligence to lower-class white children, to Spanish-speaking children, or to ghetto black children, find low IQ scores among these children, and, thus, exclude them from participation in many important institutions of our society. In 1972 a group of black parents won a decision in a class action suit against the California State Department of Education, which will enjoin the Department of Education from requiring the use of standard tests of intelligence in the assessment of black children. William Pierce, a spokesman for this group, noted, "The use of tests which are culturally biased consistently and systematically underestimate black children's intellectual potential. The use of these tests damages the child by limiting his educational opportunities" (Moriarty, 1972). Evidence of this damage is reflected by the overrepresentation of black children in classes for the mentally retarded. Although less than 10 percent of school-age children in California are black, over 27 percent are in special classes.

The Federal Court decision in California may start a trend away from the use of psychological tests as a basis for classification and diagnosis. For some psychologists this may not be a welcome decision, but for most it will be an incidental matter, since they have long ago recognized that diagnostic tests represent only a small part of the diagnostic procedure. In fact, many clinical psychologists emphasize the importance of their own observations of patients' behaviors and symptoms in the assignment of a patient to a diagnostic category.

Even in the area of mental retardation, some experts (Delay, Pichot and Perse, 1952) contend that IQ tests and intellectual performance should not be the sole basis for diagnosis. More specifically, they suggest that adequate intellectual functioning does not preclude mental retardation. Furthermore, a good intelligence quotient may be merely a ruse to hide social incompetence (a vital component of mental retardation). The diagnosis, then, of a socially incompetent person with an adequate IQ score would be "camouflaged mental deficiency."

The job of the diagnostician is, thus, a difficult and complex task. He must somehow sort out the symptoms among numerous patients and then categorize and label these symptoms, all the while maintaining a detached, objective, scientific posture. By now we are familiar with how impossible a task this is. Numerous studies have been conducted that demonstrate wide disagreement between trained observers (psychologists and psychiatrists) in the diagnosis of psychiatric disorders (see Ash, 1949; Beck, 1962; Kreitman, 1961; Schmitt & Fonda, 1956). Moreover, it has been observed (Zigler & Phillips,

1961) that even among patients with different diagnoses there is a great deal of overlap in the symptoms they present. Given these obstacles, on what basis, then, are diagnostic judgments made?

The Diagnosis of "Diagnosis"

Fifteen years ago, Hollingshead and Redlich (1958) demonstrated precisely how amenable psychiatric diagnosis is to personal and social-class bias. In particular, they found that lower-class people are over-represented in the diagnostic category of schizophrenia, while the middle-class mentally ill are usually labeled psychoneurotic. The implications of the bias for the diagnostic enterprise was not explicated until very recently. Now, two studies (not an overwhelming number to be sure) have been conducted that directly investigate the relationship between social class and diagnostic outcome.

Lee (1968) presented to diagnosticians an intensive interview, containing no elements of psychopathology, between a doctor and a "patient." By varying the biographic history, some observers were led to believe that the "patient" was lower class, while others were led to believe that he was upper class. The results showed that when the "patient" was described as lower class, he was judged more mentally ill and given a poorer prognosis than when the very same "patient" was presented as upper class.

In a more complex experiment Efron (1970) presented psychiatrists with one of three tape recorded monologues. The monologues, performed by a male actor, were designed to portray either very mild, moderate, or severe psychopathology. In addition, two biographical sketches were constructed, one depicting an upper-class man earning over $25,000 a year and the other depicting a lower-class man earning less than $5,000 a year. Before listening to one of the three tapes, each psychiatrist was presented with one of the two sketches. In total, then, one of the six combinations were presented to the psychiatrists:

Upper-class "Patient" with (1) Mild, (2) Moderate, (3) Severe Psychopathology.
Lower-class "Patient" with (4) Mild, (5) Moderate, (6) Severe Psychopathology.

After reading the biographical sketch and listening to the taped monologue, each psychiatrist was asked to evaluate the patient in terms of diagnosis, severity of disturbance, and prognosis.

Here, as in the proceeding study, the most salient feature was social-class status. In fact, the lower-class patient, regardless of the severity of the symptoms he presented, was consistently judged to be extremely psychotic with a very poor prognosis. Differential diagnosis in terms of the symptoms presented occurred only for the upper-class patient. But here, too, a bias was discernible. The most severely pathological upper-class patient received ratings identical with the most mildly pathological lower-class patient.

The relationship between social class and mental retardation has also been noted. What is lacking, however, are studies similar to those presented above to explicate the extent to which this bias operates. Nonetheless, the President's Panel on Mental Retardation (1962) has focused clearly on the link between human squalor and misery, and intellectual "defects":

> The majority of the mentally retarded are the children of the more disadvantaged classes of our society. This extraordinarily heavy prevalence in certain deprived population groups suggests a major causative role, in some way not yet fully delineated, for adverse social, economic, and cultural factors. These conditions may not only mean absence of the physical necessities of life, but the lack of opportunity and motivation. (pp. 8–9)

If social class, presumably irrelevant to intrapsychic processes, is such a potent determinant of diagnostic assignments, what other presumably irrelevant factors influence the labeling process? In part, because of the findings of our research with "defective" populations (see Braginsky, Braginsky & Ring, 1969; Braginsky & Braginsky, 1971), and also because of our observations of the current political scene, we turned our attention to political attitudes. Earlier in this book, we mentioned some of the political uses of psychodiagnosis (the en masse diagnosis of Goldwater, the Medvedev case in the U.S.S.R., etc.). These instances, however, are blatant transgressions of the ethical principles to which most mental health professionals in this country are devoted. Our concern, therefore, was with more realistic encounters between patients and diagnosticians (e.g., interview situations), encounters which often directly affect the patients' daily lives (e.g., ground privileges, discharges, etc.).

Following the logic dictated by the research concerning social-class bias and diagnosis, we anticipated that patients who express political attitudes that are very different from those of the mental health professionals would be judged to be more mentally disturbed than patients with attitudes similar to those of the professionals. Moreover, we expected that hospitalized mental patients would, in fact, have politically "deviant" attitudes (the rationale for this expectation will be explicated shortly).

In our first study (Braginsky, Braginsky & Edwards, in preparation), we administered a political attitude questionnaire designed to measure New Left Philosophy and Radical Tactics (see Christie, et al. 1969) to 100 hospitalized mental patients (50 men and 50 women) and to 50 mental health professionals at the same institution. New Left Philosophy was assessed by agreement or disagreement with statements such as: "If men were free to do what they want, then they would be happy"; "Social institutions like the church, the courts and the government need to be changed"; and so on. The Radical Tactics scores were based on responses to statements such as: "A mass revolutionary party should be created"; "You learn more in 10 minutes at a political rally than 10 hours in the library"; etc. The New Left scale is designed to assess a political philosophy emphasizing social changes, whereas the Radical Tactics scale measures political strategies to accomplish the social changes.

On both of these measures the mental patients scored significantly higher than the mental health professionals. The patients, in fact, received higher scores than Columbia University students, who prior to this had been the highest scoring sample on New Left Philosophy and Radical Tactics. Among the professionals, the social workers were the highest scorers, then the nurses and aides, and finally, the most politically conservative group, the psychiatrists and psychologists. There were no differences between the psychiatrists and the psychologists on either scale.

We have established that mental patients are politically "deviant," but it remains to be seen whether or not their deviant political attitudes influence the diagnoses they receive. Our second study, therefore, was designed to determine what relationship, if any, exists between political attitudes and diagnostic labels (Braginsky, Braginsky & Fitzgerald, in preparation). Two videotaped interviews between a doctor and a bogus mental patient (enacted by a college senior) were constructed, each of which was composed of four distinct segments: Segment 1, presenting complaints; Segment 2, expression of political philosophy; Segment 3, expression of political strategy; Segment 4, evaluative comments about mental health professions. For both interviews, the first segment was identical, consisting of complaints made by the patient in response to the doctor's question, "How are you feeling?" The complaints were typical of mildly neurotic persons (e.g., listlessness and fatigue, poor appetite, restless sleep patterns, irritability with friends).

In the second segment of the tape, the patient expressed either a New Left political philosophy or a middle-of-the-road political philosophy. In the third segment, the patient expressing the New Left attitudes endorsed the use of radical tactics to bring about social change, while the moderate patient decried the use of such strategies. Both patients in the fourth, and final, segment criticized the mental health professionals, but did so from very different perspectives. The New Left Radical accused them of being the handmaidens of a repressive society, labeling, drugging, and incarcerating anyone who disagreed with mainstream values. The middle-of-the-road patient charged that mental health professionals have done more harm to people than good by destroying traditional values, by encountering permissiveness, and by being, in general, too radical.

Each videotaped interview was shown (on separate occasions, of course) to an audience of mental health professionals who were asked to diagnose the patient and to describe the severity of his illness after each of the four segments. Thus, after Segment 1 was shown, the video-recorder was stopped, the observers completed their ratings, turned the page of their test booklet, Segment 2 was shown, and so on through Segment 4.

The results of this study, represented in Figure 3, clearly indicate the significant effect political attitudes have on psychodiagnosis. As our New Left Radical patient's complaints shift from his own person to society, he is seen as increasingly psychologically disturbed. When he suggests action to be taken to correct what is wrong with society, he is perceived as still more pathological. The moderate counterpart's psychopathology

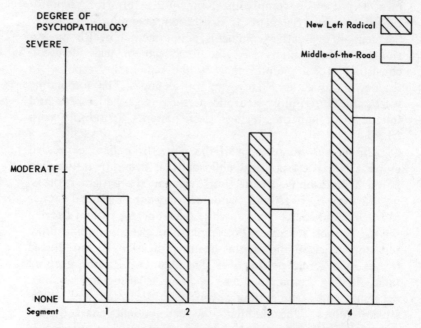

Figure 3.   Psychopathology ratings and political ideology.

remains stable as he vocalizes anti-New Left sentiments, and somewhat decreases when he criticizes those who would radically change our social institutions. Both the New Left and the middle-of-the-road patient dramatically increase in severity when they criticize mental health professionals. Even the politically "rational" young man seen as moderately disturbed (despite being presented as a hospitalized mental patient) is then diagnosed as being quite psychotic following his "irrational" attack on the mental health profession.

Indeed, the most spectacular change in the perception of the patient occurs when he directs his derogatory remarks to mental health personnel. The question that immediately comes to mind is: What happens if the patient vocalizes flattering comments? That is, if his insults are seen as a function of a "paranoid" mind, could it be conceivable that his compliments might be the function of a "normal" mind? Returning to the videorecorder, a new fourth segment was constructed that accentuated the positive and eliminated the negative aspects of mental health professionals. This new Segment 4 was used as a replacement for the New Left Radical interview. Another group of hospital staff was convened and the same procedure followed.

The results for the first three segments paralleled those obtained before. On Segment 4, however, the very disturbed mental patient was suddenly "cured" of his mental illness— a complete remission of his symptoms and a new-found normalcy. Very simply, the cure consisted of telling the doctors, social workers, nurses, and aides that they were helpful, kind, competent, and, in general, very special people.

Evidence exists, moreover, that additional, more extraneous factors also influence the assessment of the "mental state" of individuals. For instance, Wenger and Fletcher (1969) conducted a study to determine the effects, if any, of the presence of legal counsel on the outcome of commitment hearings. Mental health professionals contend that persons recommended for commitment to state mental hospitals are so obviously, demonstrably "ill" that legal intervention would not make a difference in the outcomes of the proceedings. Nonetheless,

Wenger and Fletcher, after observing eighty-one commitment hearings, discovered a strikingly high and significant correlation (.94) between the presence of a lawyer and being released. Moreover, when they controlled for "sanity" to counter the possibility that those who brought lawyers to the hearing were, in fact, "saner" than those without legal counsel, they still found that the outcome was very strongly influenced by the presence (or absence) of legal counsel.

It is clear that psychodiagnosis, even in extreme cases, is susceptible to distortion as a function of extraneous personal attributes such as social class and political ideology, in addition to extraneous situational factors such as legal intervention. Yet, it is still possible for proponents of the psychodiagnostic enterprise to contend that these criticisms, although indicating the extent to which human judgment may be distorted, do not invalidate psychodiagnostic categories. That is, there is nothing wrong with the classification schema but there is, at times, something wrong with those who use it. They might further suggest that research of the type previously cited may be very useful to psychodiagnosticians who may, as a result of the insights provided, become aware of the human errors and be on guard against them. For example, they might recommend that diagnoses be made prior to obtaining information concerning the social status and political attitudes of the person in question. Let us examine, then, the veracity of this position.

The Diagnosis of Diagnostic Labels

The process of classification is one of the first steps in the evolution of a science. By assigning the objects to be studied to groups within a system of categories, the scientist is able to focus his attention and concentrate his efforts in a meaningful and systematic fashion. The system of categories must, however, be based upon and distinguished by the structure, origin, process, and other attributes of those objects under observation.

Thus, from the earliest days of psychiatry and clinical psychology, professionals have formulated and reformulated their classifications. Manuals have been compiled (see APA,

1952; Heber, 1959) to assist the diagnostician in his labeling activities, providing categories presumably based upon "symptoms" or characteristics that *reside in* the person being diagnosed. The manuals, as well as the use of them, are based on the assumption that we can distinguish deviant, defective people from normal, effective people (e.g., the mentally ill from the sane, the mentally retarded from the intelligent). Furthermore, fine subclassifications are believed to be distinguishable (e.g., the schizophrenias, manic-depressive psychoses, psychoneuroses, morons, imbeciles, idiots). As we noted earlier, the subclassification diagnoses have been shown to be excessively unreliable (Ash, 1949; Kreitman, 1961). But what about the general distinctions between the mad and the sane, the stupid and the smart—are these valid classifications?

Do we, today, after a rather depressing history of discarded conceptions of mental illness and abandoned methods of treatment, have assurance that our present views are any more enlightened and efficacious? Scheff (1966) responds to this query with a sense of disquietude:

> Although the last five decades have seen a vast number of studies of functional mental disorder, there is as yet no substantial, verified body of knowledge in this area. At this writing there is no rigorous knowledge of the cause, cure, or even the symptoms of functional mental disorders. Such knowledge as there is, is clinical and intuitive, and thus not subject to verification by scientific methods . . . Many investigators, not only in the field of schizophrenia, but from all the studies of functional mental disorder, apparently now agree that not only have systematic studies failed to provide answers to the problem of causation, but there is considerable feeling that the problem itself has not been formulated correctly. (pp. 7–9)

Many observers of the mental health field have similarly indicted current conceptions of psychological disorders (Haley, 1969; Laing, 1967; Leifer, 1969; Sarbin, 1967; Szasz, 1961, 1963, 1970). Moreover, following an extensive, systematic program of research on mental illness (in particular, schizophrenia) we concluded that psychodiagnostic labels and their ancillary conceptions are not only misconstructions of reality but also are misleading and obfuscating. Specifically, diagnostic categories tell us nothing about the persons who are assigned to them, and their use encourages professionals to *think* they understand the disorders. This prevents us from looking further into the problems and suffering that beset many human beings (see Braginsky, Braginsky & Ring, 1969).

What about distinguishing the mentally retarded from the normal? It would appear that this should be a simpler matter. Here, too, we find conceptual chaos and unreliable and invalid definitions. A quarter of a century ago, Kanner (1948) commented:

> The casual observer may be forgiven for feeling puzzled at the groping of men and women deservedly acknowledged as experts. It does indeed seem strange that after nearly a century of scientific occupation with "feeblemindedness" those best informed should still be wondering what they have been, and are dealing with. (pp. 36–37)

More recently, Heber (1962) summarized the status of the definition of mental retardation:

> We have definitions cast in the language of the psychiatrist, neurologist, pediatrician, geneticist, sociologist, psychologist and educator. Many of these definitions are at variance with one another. Volumes of the *American Journal of Mental Deficiency* are replete with statements expounding the merits or demerits of various concepts of retardation. (p. 70)

Even the highly prestigious President's Panel on Mental Retardation (1962) could not extricate itself from this conceptual morass. In their report they refer to mental retardation as a *disease entity*, a health problem; later, they define the term as a *culturally relative concept;* and still later, as a *hypothetical construct*. But it would appear to be illogical that one concept could be real, relative, and hypothetical at the same time.

It is no wonder, then, that in our research (Braginsky & Braginsky, 1971) with cultural-familial retardates we found nothing in their behavior, their attitudes, or their life styles that could legitimately be called defective, inept, or stupid. Rather, it appears that in the entire diagnostic enterprise it is the labelers rather than the recipients who suffer from poor reality testing and defective intellectual processes.

In short, the examination of diagnostic labels in terms of historical, linguistic, and empirical analyses makes it clear that these labels tell us nothing about the recipients, but instead reveal a great deal about diagnosticians and the society that they serve.

Diagnoses as Stereotypes

To return to an earlier theme presented in this chapter, deviance is in the eye of the beholder; it is not a "property inherent in certain forms of behavior" (Erickson, 1962). The classification of deviant behavior, be it affective, cognitive, or social, cannot, therefore, be given the status of a scientific, objective endeavor. Diagnostic labels do not reflect salient characteristics of the person who is observed, but, instead, reflect the ideology and the value premises of the observer. As such, diagnoses represent nothing more than a translation of stereotypes and prejudgments about other people.

Stereotypes and prejudgments are not the invention of psychology but are probably as old as the human race, itself. Psychology has, however, added a new dimension to these age-old phenomena. It has taken the negatively valued stereotypes of society and has articulated them into diagnostic categories based on a pseudoscientific classificatory scheme. On the other hand, the positively valued social stereotypes have been translated and jargonized into "normalcy" or "mental health." Any violation of positive social values, therefore, potentially places the violater into some diagnostic category.

Thus, society has encouraged professional research psychologists to improve its stereotypes through "scientific" research on populations who they assume will meet society's negative prejudgments (the destitute, the poor, the marginal). Furthermore, professional clinical psychologists, licensed by society, are encouraged, indeed employed, to formally apply these stereotypes in the name of psychodiagnosis. The handmaiden functions of psychology are twofold here: (1) it legitimizes stereotypes as "scientific knowledge"; and (2) it assists society in "keeping its house in order" by identifying and labeling those who do not "fit in."

It is no surprise, then, to discover that most people who are formally diagnosed as deviants and who are institutionalized for treatment of their deviancy come from the lower socio-economic strata of society. Typically, they are people who add little to society's productive capacity, the "surplus populations" (Farber, 1968); as such, they are incapable of or excluded from participation in mainstream society.

The birthright of the members of surplus populations is deviancy—to be identified as a surplus person is to be labeled "deviant." Other cultures at various times in history have testified to the ease with which people may become deviants— one simply had to be born white or black, Catholic or Jew, and so on. The stigmatization and stereotyping of the surplus population requires that the meaning of their behavior be mis-construed. Thus, we find that any behaviors associated with surplus populations, behaviors often valued by their own sub-culture, are viewed by psychologists as "stupid," "irrational," "impulsive," "destructive," and "immature."

Even behaviors associated with mainstream society, when performed by the surplus population, take on a negative valua-tion. For instance, gambling by a member of the surplus popu-lation is, no doubt, an index of his immaturity and ignorance, a function of his impulsivity and inability to defer gratification, and a mark of his potential criminality. Gambling, often for much higher stakes, by a middle-class person, no doubt, attests to his sportsman-like posture, his ability to take and enjoy risks, and his love of excitement. Similarly, achievement by a Jew may be perceived as a function of his (possibly genetically determined) shrewdness and cunning, whereas achievement by a non-Jew may be seen as a sign of his intellectual gifts, social responsibility, and wholesome, masculine drive. Like-wise, a successful woman executive may be seen as castrating, aggressive, unfeminine, and disturbed, while her male counter-part is just doing what is expected of him.

Of course, there are many instances of mainstream people acquiring diagnostic labels and losing, therefore, their place in mainstream society. Here, an additional step is necessary in the labeling process, since this classification is not a birthright of mainstream populations. Thus, a middle-class person, in order to be diagnosed schizophrenic, must exhibit more severe symptoms than a member of the surplus population. The study cited earlier by Efron (1970) is an excellent example of just how difficult it is for middle-class people to obtain a stigmatizing diagnosis (also see Hollingshead & Redlich, 1958; Lee, 1968). But, as with all stereotypical labels, once obtained, it is very difficult to remove.

Rosenhan (1973) in his brilliant study, "On Being Sane in Insane Places," demonstrates further the prejudgmental, stereotypical nature of psychodiagnoses. He and seven associates obtained admission to psychiatric hospitals by telling the doctor that they heard a voice say "hollow," "empty," and "thud." Once they reported hearing these voices, there was nothing they could do to convince the staff that they were not schizophrenic. Regardless of the normalcy of their behavior, their daily comportment on the wards, and their life histories, the best they could do was to obtain a new diagnosis of schizophrenic "in remission." This meant that they were still schizophrenic, but their symptoms were not showing. Besides the "stickiness" of the label, other serious consequences of being psychodiagnosed were also explored by Rosenhan: deindividuation and powerlessness. These, again, are reminiscent of characteristics shared by other negatively stereotyped groups. They are treated as nonpeople, their individuality lost in the overpowering portrayal of the group to which they belong. Their powerlessness at overcoming the stereotype is mirrored in all their confrontations with mainstream society.

As William James once stated, "The most immutable barrier in nature is between one man's thoughts and another's." When two people trust each other and treat each other as equals, this barrier may be breached by each sharing with the other his experiences, his thoughts, and his feelings. They will attempt to articulate or otherwise communicate as much accurate information as possible. If, on the other hand, as in the diagnostic session, we have two people whose relationship is not based on trust and friendliness but is based, instead, on an inequitable power differential, little information is shared and the barrier between them grows even more immutable. Even if the powerless party in the relationship (the patient) trusts and, therefore, gives information to the other (the doctor), it is extremely unlikely to be received in the form it was intended. After all, the patient *by definition* is not a trustworthy source. Thus, the diagnostician unwillingly places himself in a position that not only precludes understanding but assures distortion and obfuscation, thinking all the while that he (as a result of his training and experience) is capable of knowing people better than they know themselves.

Labeling and Cleaning House

The diagnostic enterprise does not end with the assignment of labels. Indeed, the label is but the first step in helping to keep society's house in order. The identification and classification of deviants is not an academic exercise, but, instead, starts the rather elaborate process of social sanitation—of removing the deviants from mainstream society (see Braginsky & Braginsky, 1971). Garfinkel (1956) characterizes the outcomes of degradation processes such as psychodiagnosis: "What he is now is what, 'after all,' he was all along . . . the denounced person must be ritually separated from a place in the legitimate order . . . he must be placed outside."

In terms of the psychodiagnostic process, the labeled (denounced) person is "ritually separated" by being placed outside of society in either mental institutions or institutions for the mentally retarded. There are, of course, other institutions to house society's misfits (prisons, reformatories, orphanages), but psychologists play less of a role (although it is increasing) in them. The social sanitation process, regardless of the eventual institution, is clothed in a humanistic, "correctional stance" (see Matza, 1969). That is, the misfits are being removed from the mainstream not only to protect society but to "correct" or to somehow "treat" their problem, which is for the most part intrapsychic. Let us turn to these correctional or therapeutic activities of psychology and investigate the clinical technology of correcting deviant humans.

SEVEN

Psychotherapy

The psychodiagnostic enterprise has many ramifications, some of which we have already indicated: personal deindividuation, powerlessness, and social sanitation. Yet, there are still other ramifications that have a more direct bearing on professional psychology and its clinical technology. Specifically, the use of a highly specialized diagnostic language not only completely misconstrues the problems confronting people but translates these problems into ones that only psychologists appear to be best equipped to solve. If a woman, for example, who is extremely dissatisfied with both her husband and their marriage goes to an attorney, a divorce or a legal separation might be suggested as a solution. If, on the other hand, she takes this same problem to a psychologist, she would probably be told she was neurotic. The solution to her problem, which no longer is her marriage or her husband but, instead, might be construed as her inability to relate to men, her immaturity, or her reluctance to accept responsibility, would probably be psychotherapy.

Diagnostic labels convey the impression that the recipient

is afflicted with some disorder that renders him helpless and ineffectual in dealing with his own affairs (why otherwise would he have come to a psychologist?). Therefore, he is in need of psychotherapy. The portrayal of the "patient" as someone in whom and to whom things happen has been so widely publicized that for many persons psychodiagnostic labels become self-fulfilling prophecies. As Rosenhan (1973) notes:

> Such labels, conferred by mental health professionals, are as influential on the patient as they are on his relatives and friends, and it should not surprise anyone that the diagnosis acts on all of them as a self-fulfilling prophecy. Eventually, the patient himself accepts the diagnosis, with all of its surplus meanings and expectations, and behaves accordingly. (p. 254)

Among those things expected of the person is that he participate in some form of therapy. Here, society's desire to assist its mentally deranged citizens should be underscored. At the urging of mental health professionals, in addition to state mental hospitals, multimillion dollar community mental health centers and other facilities have been funded in order to increase the accessibility of therapy to the millions of people who "need" it. The beneficiaries of these new facilities, however, are not just the "mentally disordered" but those who service them as well. The lucrative nature of these benefits to the professionals has caused some psychologists to question, on these grounds alone, the validity of the psychodiagnostic enterprise. Graziano (1972) has paused and wondered aloud:

> Might we not, in effect, be mobilizing our social power to convince more and more persons that they are mentally ill? . . . Is it true, as Jerome Frank suggests, that the mental health establishment is one of the few professions that helps to generate its own clientele? (p. 18)

A number of mental health professionals have, in fact, interpreted the genesis of the perpetual conflict between psychologists and psychiatrists in economic terms (see Leifer, 1969, and London, 1964). The role of psychologists in the treatment of the mentally disturbed has been complicated by the medical profession, which insists that mental disorders are diseases and, as such, should be treated only by psychiatrists. Many psychologists have circumvented these charges by removing the deviant from the medical model, placing him, instead, in some psychological model such as social learning theory, operant conditioning theory, or social exchange theory. The position psychologists advocate would, in effect, improve their present status with respect to psychiatrists.

On the other hand, when it serves their best interests to endorse the medical model, psychologists seem to have few reservations about doing just that. Arthur Brayfield (1966), a former executive officer of the American Psychological Association, has been moved to comment upon this conceptual inconsistency:

. . . psychologists may reconceptualize the problem of mental health and make explicit their independent and unique role. This is the case when psychology focuses upon the developmental approach to *psychological fitness,* to *human effectiveness,* or to *social competence* in place of the medical model of illness or disease . . .

Interestingly . . . the other recent APA "White Paper" on *The Psychologist in Voluntary Health Insurance,* illustrates our inconsistency with respect to our role as a health profession. The community mental health paper espouses a nonmedical model and casts doubt on individual psychotherapy as a major approach; the insurance paper essentially accepts the medical model and the utility of one-to-one psychotherapy. (p. 1121)

Psychologists have established more than a foothold in the field of psychotherapy. Although psychiatrists are still considered the primary source for treatment, psychologists play a substantial role in therapy. They are not only able to conduct private psychotherapy (a privilege they have enjoyed for many years), but they are now considered legitimate practitioners by most major medical insurance companies. In addition, an increasing number of mental institutions are turning over more responsibility to staff psychologists than ever before (e.g., running treatment programs, being in charge of entire wards or buildings). Despite psychiatry's strenuous lobbying efforts to disenfranchise psychologists, psychology now enjoys wide acceptance, in part, as a result of the innovative therapies that they have brought with them to the clinical setting.

Finally, after years of emulating the medical profession's techniques of psychotherapy (mostly insight and psychoanalysis), psychologists now have their own therapies based on techniques found in laboratory research. Since our concern here is with psychology, we will focus upon those techniques psychology has added to the therapeutic situation. The insight psychotherapies will not be discussed for several reasons. First, the progenitor of all modern insight therapies, Freud's psychoanalysis, is the dominant orientation in contemporary psychiatry and, after numerous assaults upon its "scientific value," has been rejected by most psychologists. Although some psychologists have developed their own insight therapies (e.g., Carl Rogers' nondirective, client-centered therapy), their communalities with psychoanalysis, as London (1964) notes, overshadow their many, superficial differences.

The participants in this form of psychotherapy are atypical and represent only a small fraction of persons involved in therapy. In a study of persons who are in analysis, for instance, Weintraub and Aronson (1968) found that the typical patient is a reasonably prosperous (median income $12,500), white (100%), well-educated (over 50% hold postgraduate degrees), male (63%), professional (45%), in his thirties (over 50%), and likely to be Jewish (40%; 33% Protestant). This is hardly the portrait of the social deviants who represent by far the largest group of recipients or consumers of psychotherapy.

Insight therapies are vastly different in many ways from the therapies applied to social deviants. Here, perhaps because of the nature of the clientele, therapy is viewed as performing an educative function rather than one of social control or resocialization. As Leifer (1969) remarks:

The educative model . . . is more dignified . . . the therapeutic transaction consists of a relatively harmless exchange of information, the patient speaks freely of his history, thoughts, dreams, and activities, and the therapist reveals to him hidden aspects of self. The insight that he gains will enable the patient to be a whole person, better integrated, more able to actualize his potential, and more able to participate creatively in social relationships. (p. 171)

In short, although far more costly, participating in an insight therapy is analogous to being enrolled as a student in an adult education program. Unlike the instructor, however, the therapist is not the agent of a community nor is he empowered to exercise social control in order to mold the "student." Strict guidelines concerning the conduct of the therapist exist, among them a disavowal of social control and an affirmation of confidentiality. "The therapist must not communicate about the patient with anyone but the patient . . ." (Leifer, 1969).

Thus, the privileged status of the recipients of insight therapy is reflected in the nature of the therapeutic relationship. They are treated with the dignity and respect usually accorded to a paying customer.

Psychology's Psychotherapies

Psychology's contribution to the psychotherapeutic situation is mostly comprised of techniques based upon the laboratory theories of Pavlov, Hull, Thorndike, and Skinner, which have been brought to clinical settings by, among others, Wolpe, Stampfl, and, of course, Skinner. Some tentative moves have been made by the humanists in this area, but the therapeutic field in psychology is dominated by the behaviorists. They have evolved what London (1964) calls action therapies. The process and goal is for the therapist to "*manipulate stimulus-response connections* in order deliberately *to change specific behavior* from one pattern of activity to another" (London, 1964; italics ours). Exactly how they manipulate the S–R connections and the behaviors that they deliberately attempt to change will be detailed shortly. Before that exploration, however, a brief look at some of the differences between insight and action therapies would be valuable.

The recipients of action therapies are, for the most part, from a much lower social stratum than the recipients of insight therapies. In addition, action therapy is most frequently conducted in institutional or bureaucratic settings (mental hospitals, training schools, etc.) with patients who are often placed in these programs on the basis of administrative rather than personal decisions. Moreover, the therapist, acting in these settings as an agent of the community, the state, or the family, perceives his task not in the educative model but in the moralizing model. That is, the therapist is given the social power to formally manipulate the patient so that his behavior will conform to the prevailing social norms. Or as Leifer (1969) phrases it: "It is indoctrination or training for culturally specific traits, attitudes, and actions."

Briefly, then, compared to insight therapies, the action therapies of psychology: (1) are not transactional (i.e., there is no exchange of information between patient and therapist); (2) are explicitly manipulative and controlling; (3) are based upon goals set by mainstream social norms (i.e., indoctrinating); (4) are rarely voluntarily engaged in by patients (although no one, we are sure, would be *forced* to participate); and (5) are, in general, humiliating and undignified encounters. In short, action therapies are tailored for the consumption of the poor, the powerless, and the "misfits."

Once, again, we find psychology permeated with sociopolitical-economic value premises in the guise of scientific theories. In the psychotherapeutic enterprise, as we will soon see, these mainstream values are promoted as the objectives of therapy. Thus, psychologists have entered a region of human interaction that had been characterized by dignity, respect, privacy, and freedom of expression. Yet, in addition to their therapeutic methods, they have brought the social inequities, the robotization (and "dehomunculization") of man, and the emphasis on what man does (behavior) rather than what he is that have characterized the psychological research laboratory. The barrenness and mythology of the empirical enterprise in psychology can only be matched by its therapeutic activities.

What Is Psychotherapy?

Psychotherapy, in general, is entirely dependent upon its goals and techniques for its definition. The goals, as we have seen, may be either educative or moralizing, and the techniques are either insight or action oriented. There are, of course, therapies that utilize various combinations of these goals and techniques. Nonetheless, there is no definition of psychotherapy that goes beyond its operations and intentions.

The point might be raised that since psychotherapy is an umbrella-like concept, embracing a diversity of theories and techniques, a precise definition is impossible. Yet, in a restrictive, ritualized form of therapy such as psychoanalysis, a definition could not even be arrived at after a four-year American Psychoanalytic Association subcommittee study. There was, however, agreement on who should be allowed to practice psychoanalysis: "medical training iş an indispensable prerequisite for the practice of psychoanalysis . . ." (London, 1964). An exception was explicitly made for those who trained in Vienna before 1937 in order to include luminaries without medical degrees, such as Anna Freud and Theodore Reik.

A statement made by a participant at a conference on clinical psychology's therapy training, summarized by Victor Raimy, wryly describes the current state: *"Psychotherapy is an undefined technique applied to unspecified cases with unpredictable results. For this technique, rigorous training is required"* (in London, 1964).

Although psychotherapy can at best be described as that which psychotherapists do (and there is no agreement upon what it is that they do), there is, nevertheless, unanimity concerning who should be allowed to practice it. Thus, extensive training programs have evolved, and certification and licensing procedures have been carefully detailed. But the inability to concur on a definition raises very serious questions regarding acceptable standards of performance. As Leifer (1969) remarks, "How can a professional group regulate an activity it is unable to define . . . ? The answer, obviously, is that it cannot." Unlike the performance of any other professional group (lawyers, surgeons, dentists, chiropractors), the performance of psychotherapists remains largely unregulated.

There is little cause for alarm since the conduct of most psychotherapists falls within the acceptable range of behavior and propriety norms of society. Indeed, when professionals deviate from these norms, extraprofessional measures (usually civil or criminal law) may be employed to control the therapists' conduct. The harrassment and imprisonment of Wilhelm Reich over twenty years ago for violating propriety norms (which today seem prudish) is one rather tragic instance of societal intervention. But as restrictions placed upon ordinary citizens are loosened, so, too, are the limits imposed on psychotherapists. Today, therapists engage in behaviors that just five years ago might have led to legal action, if not imprisonment.

Psychologists as psychotherapists have one additional limitation placed upon them: they may not violate the territory of medical professional groups (e.g., they cannot prescribe or administer drugs, perform psychosurgery, or conduct electroshock treatment). Aside from these medical activities, any method from smiling to having sexual intercourse with a client is permissible for licensed or certified psychotherapists. This does not mean that controversy concerning techniques do not exist in the profession (or malpractice suits brought by dissatisfied clients). In recent years, the literature dealing with psychotherapy has abounded with outcries against or advocacies for various techniques. Let us turn now to the technique based upon "scientific" psychological theory and research.

Might Makes Right:
Behavior Modification

The technique that has captured the imagination of today's clinical psychologists in ever increasing numbers, particularly those in institutional settings, falls under the heading of "behavior modification." As the name implies, this therapeutic endeavor is scientifically rooted in behaviorism and is, perhaps, the only therapy that grew out of laboratory work in highly controlled situations with animals. The goals of behavior shaping, the use of positive and negative reinforcers, the

Law of Reinforcement and Extinction, and all the other techniques of behaviorism (including its Calvinistic ideology) have been applied to the clinical setting.

Two proponents of behavior modification, Schaefer and Martin (1969), have made explicit the similarities between the laboratory and their own therapeutic endeavors:

> In clinical psychotherapy . . . the objective is to change unacceptable behaviors to acceptable behaviors. But many traditional therapists go to great lengths to make sure it is understood that they are in no way controlling either their patient's outlook on life or his behavior . . . The behavioral therapist, on the other hand, is *not beset by such fears.* He recognizes that *he controls the behavior* of those who come to him for help, regardless of whether he wants to or not and, indeed, irrespective of whether or not he believes that he does. He realizes that *he is responsible* for what his patients do while they are in his care and that *he cannot hide* behind the pretense that it is up to the patients to make their own decisions to do what is "right." (p. 12; italics ours)

Only upon reading this can people become acquainted with the enormity of the load the deviant represents to the behavioral therapists. Exactly how do some of these therapists handle this burden?

Therapist as Food Pellet Dispenser

One scientific discovery made by the behavioral therapists, described by Schaefer and Martin (1969) as a central achievement, is the relationship between deprivation and behavior: ". . . a man who has starved for three days is likely to do anything for a morsel of bread. On the other hand, someone who has just finished a rich meal would hardly consider a morsel of bread a reinforcer." If the point failed to be fully appreciated, they state further: "A man who is not thirsty is unlikely to do anything just to get a drink."

It was no doubt with this discovery in mind that Kassorla (1969) conducted the following therapeutic experiment: One of the "sickest" patients in a British mental hospital was used as the subject—a catatonic, mute schizophrenic man in his early fifties who had been hospitalized for thirty-two years, during thirty of which he did not speak. Early in 1967, Kassorla and her colleagues embarked upon an operant conditioning project "based on the principle that behavior which is reinforced is likely to occur again . . ."

On the first day of the experiment the subject (Mr. B.) was asked 120 simple questions such as "What is your name?", "How old are you?" and so on. He remained silent on 89 percent of the questions. When he did respond it was usually with a soft "ugh," only twice vocalizing something sounding like "crack 'em." It was this sound "crack 'em" that was selected as the initial behavior to be reinforced. That is, the experimenter would say the word "crack 'em;" if Mr. B. repeated the word or moved his mouth even slightly, he would be reinforced. Here the experimenter encountered some difficulty with the hospital staff concerning reinforcers. As Kassorla explains:

> With our severely withdrawn patient, we could not expect intangible reinforcements to have much effect, especially at first . . . *the reinforcement we relied on was food.* In spite of considerable resistance from the hospital staff, which felt that Mr. B. was too sick to talk and should not be treated "unkindly," *we took full control of the patient's feeding.* (p. 40; italics ours)

At first, Mr. B. was given food if, after the experimenter said "crack 'em," he repeated it or he moved his lips. By day 14, Mr. B. repeated that word 92 percent of the time. As the training progressed, other words like "dog" were introduced. Later, a picture of a dog was shown to him and he was required to identify it. For seven days, however, he responded with "I don't know." The experimenters "decided that this negativistic behavior was interfering with the patient's progress and . . . deliberately set out to extinguish it." Thus, every time Mr. B. said "I don't know" when asked to identify the picture of the dog, he was removed entirely from the experimental room where he received his food. After four days he stopped saying "I don't know," giving, instead, the correct response—"dog."

The training was completed after 138 days, whereupon the same 120 questions asked of him at the onset of the project were repeated. He responded "appropriately" 75 percent of the time, which was no small achievement. As the behavioral therapists contend, their mode of treatment indeed produces results. After thirty years, Mr. B.'s speech did return. Yet, their explanation of why it returned, as well as their procedure to elicit its return, are, to say the least, questionable.

"Experts at operant conditioning," Kassorla maintains, "working in the ideal one-to-one relationship" have the task (and a difficult one it is) of "identifying approximations of *desirable behavior* in psychotics and figuring out what they will find reinforcing" (italics ours). Once this is achieved, the behavioral therapist then offers to the psychotic a "reliable schedule of positive reinforcements." The most serious misconstruction here is the perception of the experimenter–therapist as providing positive reinforcers, when, in fact, they are withholding food from the subject until he submits to the therapist's desires. In earlier times, and in other contexts, such therapeutic behavior was considered torture; as such, it represents a better explanation of reality than the behaviorists' interpretation.

That only "experts at operant conditioning" can realize that food, when a person is deprived of it, is reinforcing—if not necessary to life itself—is a notion that can be entertained by persons who have read only books by Skinner and his followers, and who have never been hungry themselves. We are certain that had the hospital staff been willing to employ succinylcholine (a drug that induces respiratory arrest for about two minutes), for example, Mr. B. would have relinquished his mute behavior long before the 138-day training period. Oxygen deprivation would have produced faster results than food deprivation. Or in the behaviorists' terms—oxygen reinforcers are more reinforcing than food reinforcers.

The behaviorists' distortions here are twofold: First, they focus upon what they give to the subject rather than what they have removed, enabling them to perceive their behavior as benevolent instead of punitive. Second, and more important, they have again taken common knowledge, knowledge used for centuries by mankind's oppressors, and have called it their "new" discovery. Since it is their discovery, then they should be the only ones licensed to use it.

Therapist as Pay Boss

A variation on the reinforcement theme, based, of course, on the vast literature in learning theory concerning animals (although identical bases may be found in any newspaper or magazine) is the "token economy" motivational system. Ayllon and Azrin (1968) conducted extensive research on hospitalized mental patients using tokens as conditioned reinforcers (in contrast to primary reinforcers, for which the tokens may be traded). The results of their program of systematic investigation showed that:

> . . . patients totally discontinued working on a previously preferred job when reinforcers were no longer forthcoming for that job . . . When reinforcement was reinstated, all patients immediately resumed the full-time job for which the reinforcers were being given. These results show that the reinforcement was the major and almost exclusive reason why the patients were performing their jobs. (p. 187)

Further refinements of their procedure produced similar *discoveries,* such as: If tokens were given to the patients before their job performance, the performance decreased; patients desired those jobs that yielded the most tokens rather than jobs giving a smaller number of tokens; the patients were exchanging all the tokens they had for reinforcers (primary ones). Encouraged by these findings, the authors concluded:

> The effectiveness of the motivating environment in maintaining the desired behaviors of the patients over this very wide range of individual differences indicates that the program succeeded in its attempt to design a total environment that could take advantage of the wide range of individual interests and preferences of an exceedingly heterogeneous population. (p. 191)

Does it appear that the behaviorists are first discovering capitalism? Once again, then, we find the behaviorists discovering the "wheel" thousands of years after everyone has been effectively using it. The naïvete of the behavioral therapists concerning token economies is surpassed only by their naïvete about the conditions of other people. For instance, Ayllon and Azrin (1968), in summarizing their results, engage in further insights concerning the mental patients: "The results are especially revealing in that the jobs used in this experiment were full-time jobs that closely approximated the type of job engaged in by normal, non-institutionalized persons and might be considered to be especially susceptible to *nonmonetary influences* such as *job satisfaction*" (italics ours). Yet, the jobs from which it was assumed normal, noninstitutionalized people would derive job satisfaction were: "Dietary worker—helps serve 85 patients and cleans tables after meals"; "Clerical—types and answers the telephone; Calls hospital personnel to the telephone"; "Laboratory—cleans cage pans, fills water bottles and cleans floor in laboratory"; "Laundry—helps to run sheets, pillow cases and towels through mangle at hospital laundry; Also fold linen."

Most people might raise an eyebrow at a companion who describes the job satisfaction he has when he cleans a cage pan, runs a towel through the mangle, calls a doctor to the telephone, or cleans off a table. The behaviorists have not yet formulated what the components of job satisfaction are. When they do, perhaps a more realistic appraisal of the work situation will be made.

In the world of industrial organizations, William F. White (1972), although agreeing with Skinner's basic formulation, discerns four crucial elements operant conditioning fails to deal with: "(1) the cost-benefit ratio and the social-comparison process; (2) the problem of conflicting stimuli; (3) the problem of time lag and trust; and (4) the one-body problem." In less sophisticated terms these are exactly the problems the labor movement has been attempting to deal with these past fifty years, although from a quite different perspective. Although Skinner does not advocate piece-rate compensation, all of the behaviorists' research points to this incentive system. This method of compensation has not only been used before, but by now has been abandoned by most civilized, fairminded industrialists. Indeed, the social engineering of the behaviorists (which we will deal with in greater detail shortly) is more like the "sweat shop" than the "brave new world."

Therapist as One-Up-Man

Despite the antiquity of most of the behaviorist methods in therapy, one genuinely innovative and provocative use of reinforcers is described by Schaefer and Martin (1969). In their chapter dealing with the treatment of "odd behaviors," they suggest that foul language, screams, and threats can be dealt with in the following manner:

> Unexpectedly being reinforced (with cigarettes, tokens, or any suitable reinforcer) for a behavior which in the past was maintained by altogether different reinforcers is apparently so shocking to some patients that after only a single reinforcement the behavior ceases. When this is not successful, a condition may be introduced whereby after each reinforcement the volume of sound must be increased to bring on the reinforcers. We have used this technique effectively under the following schedule.
>
> 1. One minute of cursing or   1. cigarette, token, etc.
>   screaming in the isolation
>   room;
> 2. Two additional minutes of   2. cigarettes, tokens, etc.
>   continuous louder cursing;
>
> The patient will often cease cursing or screaming after this event. Quiet weeping typically follows. (pp. 121–132)

This technique might be described as treating odd behavior with still stranger behavior. Imagine the astonishment of the patient when the therapists reward him following a foulmouthed tirade against them. He is left with two equally bewildering possible conclusions: either he is really sicker than he or anyone else ever thought (because this really could not have happened; he must have hallucinated it), or that the therapists are sicker than he is (which he may have in the past only suspected), leading him to a state of utter anxiety about his future welfare under the therapists' care.

The patient who does not respond immediately, but tries again to test reality (did what I think happened, really happen?) is quietly led to a seclusion room after his second outburst of profanities. There, he is given not one, but two, cigarettes. He cannot avoid the conclusion that, indeed, the therapists have become deranged. It might seem appropriate that quiet weeping should typically follow this peculiar encounter. The therapists' one-up-manship has quieted the surly, vulgar patient because it is impossible to curse aloud when one's mouth is agape or when one is weeping gently.

We are not sure how, if at all, this method fits into the scheme of behavioral modification. On the basis of laboratory studies and theory, we would predict that the cursing, under these conditions, would increase. Perhaps it just indicates how unpredictable human subjects are.

Another example of "turning the table" as a successful way of treating odd behavior involved a woman patient who hoarded about twenty towels in her room. Ayllon (1963) told the nursing staff not only to stop removing the hoarded towels from the woman's room, but to take a towel to the patient's room at varying time intervals. The number of towels taken to the room increased as the weeks went by. Finally, when the hoard of towels reached 625, the patient began to find them aversive. She said to the staff, "take them towels away!" Ayllon attributes the long-lasting curative effect to the behaviorist principle of *satiation*. It might, however, be more simply understood in terms of fear—fear of those "crazy" nurses or suffocation by towels.

Therapist as Punisher

The above manifestations of behaviorism might be appreciated on levels other than psychotherapeutic. This innocence and naïvete represents, however, only a small segment of behaviorism. The behaviorist movement's influence on clinical psychology is most clearly seen when the behavioral modifier acts as a punishment.

The most commonly employed punishing stimulus in behavioral modification is electric shock (not to be confused with electro-convulsive shock therapy used by psychiatrists). Kushner (1970), an authority on *faradic aversive controls*, describes the scientific bases of selecting electric shock for clinical practice. After an extensive review of the literature concerning noxious stimuli that have been used clinically (e.g., emetics that produce nausea and vomiting, curare-like drugs that inhibit respiration, white noise, air-blasts) he, as well as many colleagues, agree that electric shock is overall more desirable and advantageous. Specifically, electric shock contains important features such as "ease and simplicity of operation," "may be activated either automatically via programming or by the therapist," and "technicians or quasi-professional personnel can be readily trained to operate the equipment." In addition, electric shock is reasonably safe (aside from serious heart conditions), the "stimulation impinges upon the subject immediately upon activation," and the intensity is readily controllable. In short, electric shock is scientifically the ideal punisher.

Let us now see how Kushner has used faradic aversive controls in behavioral modification.

A seventeen-year-old girl had been sneezing vigorously and frequently (about once every 40 seconds) for six months with no relief. She had been to neurologists, endocrinologists, allergists, hypnotists, even psychiatrists, all to no avail. Kushner's (1970) treatment involved placing a microphone around her neck, which was connected to a voice key and a shock source. The sneezing thus activated the sound relay, which in turn triggered the electric shock that was delivered to her fingertips. Within a few hours the sneezing discontinued. But, as Kushner points out, "This case is another instance in which the aversive procedure was only the *first phase* in the total treatment program" (italics ours). Therapy talk sessions followed to help her develop more appropriate ways of dealing with her environment.

Another successful use of behavioral modification reported

by Kushner (1970) involved fetishism in a thirty-three-year-old man. At about the age of twelve when he saw, and subsequently became aroused by, little girls' panties, a life-long interest in women's undergarments was developed. He would buy panties or sometimes take them from clotheslines, put them on, and masturbate. Moreover, he was impotent in normal heterosexual relationships. The treatment program involved the presentation of the fetishistic object, pictures, and ideational stimuli followed by a brief, but uncomfortable shock. The patient was told that he could terminate the shock by saying "stop" and putting aside the fetishistic object, picture, or idea. After a period of only 14 weeks, with forty-one shock sessions (giving a total of 492 shocks), the patient reported that panties no longer aroused him. Aside from two brief relapses, (in each case the therapist gave him "booster" shocks) the patient's unwholesome interest in women's underpants seemed to have vanished. Now, with the help of the therapist (without the use of shocks) and a considerate girlfriend, the problem of the patient's impotence is being attacked.

A final illustration (Kushner, 1970) of electric shock treatment concerns the self-destructive behavior of a severely retarded seven-year-old boy. The behavior to be eliminated was hand-biting, so severe that it caused bleeding and, at times, infection. The staff used elbow splints or boxing gloves in an attempt to keep the child's hands from his mouth. The child, it was noted, also tried to hide his hands from himself by sitting on them or holding on to a nurse's hands. Although the biting behavior, reportedly, began at home, it was intensified upon hospitalization when the child was placed in a room with another child who had a rare congenital disorder that resulted in severe biting of any part of the body. The treatment for the seven-year-old boy was to attach electrodes "about the child's thigh; the shock was made contingent with hand-biting." In addition, efforts to hide his hands were also shocked. Kushner reports what happened:

During the first session there was considerable crying, frantic looking around for nursing personnel who were excluded, and constant moving about on the chair upon which he was seated. He made only one brief effort to remove the electrodes . . . (p. 44)

During that first session of 56 minutes, the child put his hands in his mouth or hid his hands approximately sixty-five times; each time he received a shock. It is noteworthy that although Kushner is meticulous in his procedural descriptions, including the intensity of the shock in other cases, here there was no mention of the strength of the shock. Two days later, when the second session was conducted, the child sat quietly, "uttered only a momentary soft cry when the shock was delivered" and appeared to be composed. During this 56-minute block of time, less than ten shocks had to be administered. The child, for the moment at least, had been encouraged not to bite his hands. Kushner notes that he was unable to continue this case, but he felt that it was instructive, nonetheless. We agree; this case was, indeed, instructive.

Since the punishment-as-therapy theme evokes the most serious criticism, we will deal with these cases in a separate section. But first, one more therapeutic role available to the behavioral therapist will be described.

Therapist as Emetic

An interesting variation of the aversive shock conditioning described above has been developed by Cautela (1971). By using the technique of covert sensitization, he has helped his patients rid themselves of maladaptive sexual behaviors (fetishism, sadism, masochism, homosexuality, rape). Cautela claims that covert sensitization has advantages over electric shock conditioning, "The use of electric shock is time-consuming, expensive, and often results in a high drop-out rate." Moreover, its practical use in *private* practice as well as its use as a self-control device is limited. In covert sensitization, however, the shock is *imaginary*.

The therapist first discovers the patient's desirable sexual objects and then constructs vivid imaginary scenes in which he confronts this desired object in a less than favorable situation. For instance, Cautela's imaginary scene for a homosexual:

> You are in a dungeon. It is dark, smelly and altogether loath-some . . . You can just barely see an attractive male nude in a corner . . . You think to yourself, "Boy, this is going to be good." As you think that, you begin to get a funny, queasy feeling in the pit of your stomach. Some chunks of food come into your mouth and taste bitter . . . Just as you're about to touch him, you start to vomit. You vomit all over him, all over yourself . . . His entire body is covered with it, especially his penis . . . He grabs for you and you trip and fall face down into a huge pile of vomit . . . As you run out the door you feel better and better. When you get out into the clean fresh air, you feel wonderful. (p. 12)

The therapist who might hesitate to use this procedure in his nicely carpeted office is assured by Cautela that not one of his patients ever became sick while undergoing treatment. According to Cautela, those patients who remained in therapy and followed the therapist's instructions, generally modified their "sexual behavior in a desirable direction." Although this technique does not precisely follow Skinner's notions, imagery might still have a place. Imagination, so long as it is the product of behaviorists, may be applied to their clients.

The Chamber of Horrors

Although we enumerated several postures that the behavioral therapist may assume, they all share in common a punitive element, regardless of the names given to the techniques we described. Every method available to the therapist involves some form of cruelty, either subtle or overt, explicit or implicit. Thus, therapy-as-punishment is not the exclusive property of the faradic aversive conditioners, although they seem to be least disquieted by this image. Indeed, in a number of position papers, behaviorists have attempted to re-educate those who object to the use of punishment for therapeutic purposes.

Baer (1970, 1971), addressing the issue of punishment,

prevails upon the fainthearted to take another look. Punishment, he reminds us, is a natural part of growing up, yet "we have a peculiar ambivalence toward pain." Specifically, pain inflicted by inanimate objects, such as sharp knives, hard floors, or hot radiators, are viewed by most people as "good teachers"; on the other hand, pain inflicted by other people is seen as "barbaric and repellent." Here, it should be noted that Baer (like all behaviorists) perceives inanimate objects as having powers to inflict punishment—a clear extension of the strange notions behaviorists have about the inanimate environment. Yet, most people might be somewhat alarmed if a friend reported that while slicing cheese the knife punished him; or, after falling off a ladder, said that the hard ground taught him a lesson.

Nonetheless, Baer recognizes that the use of punishment as a therapeutic technique does present a dilemma; not a moral one, as most people would assume, but rather a "bookkeeping" problem:

> The therapist who humanely avoids inflicting pain on his patients has no moral superiority over another therapist who gives a patient electrical punishment so that he may escape social punishment. *The basic questions are which punishment is tougher, and which lasts longer?* (p. 36; italics ours)

For the therapist who might still have qualms about this technique, Baer provides this simple formula: ". . . a small number of brief, painful experiences is a reasonable exchange for the interminable pain of a lifelong maladjustment." Thus, the good therapist, like the good Prince

> . . . must not mind incurring the charge of cruelty for the purpose of keeping his subjects united and faithful; for, with a very few examples, he will be more merciful than those who, from excess tenderness, allow disorders to arise, from whence spring bloodshed and rapine; for these as a rule injure the whole community. . . . (Machiavelli, 1950 ed., p. 60)

Although the behavioral therapists claim that it is their patients' interests that come first, they assume also an isomorphic relationship between society's and patients' interests (i.e., what is good for society is good for the patient). The "good" psychotherapist, as Baer has reminded us, is not the therapist who uses benevolent methods while his patient continues to undergo daily social punishment; instead, it is the therapist who corrects the patient's deviant habits, using whatever means available (and that includes punishment). In short, behavioral therapy in professional position papers makes explicit its moral goals to resocialize the patient, but this is never expressed to the patient. That is, patients are not made aware that the therapy goals represent a value judgment on the part of the therapist and that there are other ways to view and "treat" their problems.

The primacy of the social order in the behaviorist's view of the world has been articulated by another proponent of behavior modification, McConnell (1970). He submits that we must use whatever techniques are available in order to "build a society in which laws become guidelines rather than threats, guidelines so strong that *no one would want to do anything other than follow them. . . .* Somehow we've got to learn how to *force* people to love one another, to *force* them to behave properly" (italics ours except for *force*).

Since McConnell dismisses civil liberties and in fact, the entire system of jurisprudence in western civilizations, it is no surprise that he proposes further that we "reshape our society so that we all would be *trained from birth to do what society wants us to do*" (italics ours). By accomplishing this state of affairs, McConnell maintains, we can then hope to "maximize human potentiality." The justification for enslaving man to social norms that dominates behaviorist ideas is articulated in a frightfully clear manner by McConnell:

No one owns his own personality. Your ego, or individuality, was forced on you by your genetic constitution and by the society into which you were born. You had no say about what kind of personality you acquired, and there's no reason to believe you should have the right to refuse to acquire a new personality if your old one is antisocial. (p. 74)

It is no wonder that the behaviorists are disturbed by the extraneous, nonscientific nonsense that is "read" into their work by persons not committed to the behaviorist movement. Baer (1971) has expressed his disappointment over the almost total lack of appreciation that has accompanied the *discoveries* of the behaviorists, especially concerning punishment, "By the usual standards of science these findings ought to evoke admiration. . . . So instead of celebrating a new scientific advance, we feel apprehensive; we look for a hint of sadism."

Schaefer and Martin (1969) have also been moved to comment that, "In their eagerness to understand behavioral therapy, many well-meaning public officials will try to *draw historical parallels which are often misleading*" (italics ours). Criticisms, they say, are sometimes waged against behavior modification programs claiming that "patients are being starved into submission, much as was done in German concentration camps." The foolishness of this parallel, as Schaefer and Martin point out, is that the critics do not understand that "patients are actually rewarded with food." Their response, like those of the other behaviorists, misses the very essence of the criticism. The patients are being *rewarded* with food for submission. If they do not submit to the prescribed behaviors, they are deprived of food. Again, Schaefer and Martin, like their colleagues, have misunderstood the criticism entirely. Surely, we do not assume that the behavioral therapist would endanger the lives of his patients by a lengthy withdrawal of food. But that is not the point. The paradigm presented by the behaviorists is essentially identical both in structural and functional terms to the model used throughout history between masters and slaves, guards and prisoners, kings and serfs, Nazis and concentration camp inmates.

As a result of the behaviorists' inability to grasp the similarity of "treatment" models, they conclude that if the public was *educated* and *enlightened,* they would enthusiastically endorse behavioral modification techniques. By now, it is clear that it is not the public's lack of education that requires attention but the behaviorists'. The well-intentioned public officials (as well as other nonbehaviorists) who have drawn historical parallels, have done so because the historical parallels exist. That is, being educated and aware of the real world, they have seen the antiquity of the behaviorist methods. The behaviorists, on the other hand, have once again rediscovered and retranslated into their own ideological formula knowledge that has been available to man throughout history.

The behavioral therapists, unlike most other psychotherapists, conduct their activities in an historical and moral vacuum. They, more than any other psychotherapists, "appeal to science to justify their activity, just as ministers appeal to revelation" (London, 1964). Confident that they have discovered new, meaningful, objective, and scientific solutions to age-old problems, the behavioral therapists, when they pause to reflect upon their technology (which usually occurs after some "uninformed" attack), completely misconstrue the ramifications of their therapeutic techniques.

For the first time in the history of American psychology (or, for that matter, psychology in any democracy), professional psychologists have explicitly offered their services to the authorities in power. These services not only attempt to render deviant behavior patterns socially acceptable, but also inculcate mainstream values, mores, and taboos to make the deviant want to behave in a socially approved manner. It is obvious why behavior modification has been enthusiastically endorsed by state institutions for the mentally ill, mentally retarded, and criminal. Behaviorists offer the authorities a scientifically respectable rationale for engaging in forms of social control explicitly denied by the Constitution.

We do not mean to attack the motives of the behaviorists especially since they appear to be unaware of the implications of their theory and practices. Skinner (1971), for instance, has emphatically stated that he wants this control only to help mankind survive; to save man from the hell he is sure to end up in without scientific intervention:

Our culture has produced the science and technology it needs to save itself. It has the wealth needed for effective action. It has, to a considerable extent, a concern for its future. But *if it continues to take freedom and dignity, rather than its own survival, as its principal value,* then it is possible that some other culture will make a greater contribution to the future. The defender of freedom and dignity may then, *like Milton's Satan,* continue to tell himself that he has "a mind not to be changed by place and time" and all sufficient personal identity . . . but *he will nevertheless find himself in hell* with no other consolation than the illusion that "here at least we shall be free." (pp. 181–182; italics ours)

Skinner's hope, as well as McConnell's (1970) claim, that "Today's behavioral psychologists are the architects and engineers of the Brave New World," is unfortunately incorrect. Their proposal to create a Brave New World by removing freedom, dignity, and individuality is little more than a return to the old world that enlightened men had devoted and, often, given their lives to change. The world these behaviorists envision can be found in totalitarian states not only of the past but of today as well. The techniques of behavior control they consider so elaborate and sophisticated are amateurish attempts compared to the social control techniques of the Medici, Hitler, and Stalin. It is unfortunate that what the behaviorists have chosen to rediscover and proselytize are those very things that represent the worst in man; goals and activities that have been condemned and inhibited by religious doctrine, the legal system, labor unions, and so on.

Skinner, in a published dialogue with Evans (1968), remarked about the similarity of behavioral and totalitarian techniques. Evans, a psychologist, noted the parallels between Skinner's discussion and the formula of communications control outlined in Goebbel's diary: "Many of the techniques he described reflect the principles of reinforcement that you have written about." Skinner replied, "Oh, yes. *The Nazis made good use of the social sciences* even though they had driven out most of the good people. It was 'good' from their point of view, of course; dangerous from ours" (italics ours).

Bearing in mind the dangers inherent in the social control model they propose, the behaviorists have tried to reassure us that their techniques will be used only for "good" purposes. If their philosophical and ethical prowess is at all similar to their scientific and intellectual processes, the prospects are not pleasant. McConnell's (1970) interpretation of the Constitution (which scholars have puzzled over for years) may serve as a prelude:

> I don't believe the Constitution of the United States gives you the *right* to commit a crime if you want to; *therefore, the Constitution does not guarantee you the right to maintain inviolable the personality* it forced on you in the first place—if and when the personality manifests strongly antisocial behavior. (p. 74; italics ours except for first *right*)

As the behaviorists see it, their basic problem, then, is not how to determine appropriate behavior or the limits of the social power they should exercise. Leifer (1969) has indicated already that, "The power of the therapist is derived from the *authority of the group* that sanctions him as a healer, as a wise man of science, as an expert in human affairs, and as a man of Good, if not of God." Armed with divine right and with a technology so simple that Baer (1971) declared, "Anyone with a hand to swing is equipped with a punishing device," the behavioral therapist is cautioned to use his "might" carefully.

The pitfalls facing behavioral therapists is interpreted by Baer (1970, 1971) in this manner. Since punishment is so efficient and simple, and since inexpensive and reliable devices such as *cattle prods* facilitate the administration of punishment (for an excellent example of the use of cattle prods on autistic children, see Bucher and Lovaas, 1968), "there is the danger that it could become the first or even the exclusive technique of carelessly trained therapists." The *danger* the behaviorists perceive, however, does not concern the patient receiving the punishment. Instead, the danger is to the therapist who may, by applying punishment, acquire a punishment function himself. As Baer (1970) cautions his colleagues:

> If the person who applies punishment becomes himself a punishing stimulus for another, he should expect all the relevant behaviors: escape, avoidance and removal with respect to the stimulus. *One way to remove a social stimulus is to murder it.*

Clearly, anyone using punishment should look to his total stimulus function with great care. (p. 248)

Baer is, of course, correct. No one likes a hangman even if he is a professional psychologist. But rather than question their function as the psychic hangmen of society, the behavioral therapists are cautioned to cover their tracks with positive reinforcers or else to be prepared to be removed as a social stimulus.

Need we add more? We think not.

Behavior modification, thus, has brought us full circle in the "treatment" of the mentally deranged or behaviorally aberrant. In earlier years, the introduction of psychologists to large state institutions had a humanizing effect; patients were, while in the company of the psychologists, spoken to and listened to. The behavioral therapists' techniques have brought a new form of dehumanization ("dehomunculization") back to the asylum. Behaviorism has borrowed and supported the age-old ideologies of tyranny from which men have fought to free themselves. It is the ideological primacy (not merely the tyranny) of the behaviorist position that divorces it from the realm of science and objectivity.

Our purpose was to indicate how and what kind of ideology permeates and shapes what the behaviorists have called "psychological" theory and "scientific" therapeutic methods. Since, as we noted in the first chapter, the very heart of psychology is a moral enterprise, the behaviorists are not the only psychotherapists who clothe their beliefs in science. There do exist, however, vital differences with respect to the ideologies of the various groups.

Though the behaviorists maintain that all psychotherapists engage in some form of social control, the difference between the behavioral modifiers and most other therapists is analogous to the gulf between prison guards and parsons, policemen and theater ushers. Behavioral therapists function mostly within an institutional context, where they are endowed with greater power than in any other therapeutic setting (e.g., mental health clinic, private practice). They have the power to influence almost every aspect of the patient's life within the total institution (privileges, week-end passes, number of tokens, etc.), while the patient has no formal socially sanctioned power. Thus, the therapist *may do* what he wants with the patient in order to help him, but the patient *must do* what the therapist desires. In no other setting, then, does the therapist enjoy such complete control over his patient. Behavior therapy, therefore, is *the* therapy for treatmᵒnt of the powerless.

Not everyone, of course, who is a patient in psychotherapy is powerless. What therapies have psychologists devised apart from variants of insight therapies for those persons who occupy positions of social power? That is, besides the dignified, verbal exchange of information, what techniques have psychologists developed and what new goals have they proposed?

Humanistic Psychotherapy

Although earlier in this book we described a variety of market-place technologies associated with the humanistic movement, few would be considered by their proponents as psychotherapy. One reason why Third Force advocates avoid calling their techniques psychotherapeutic involves the limitations imposed by licensing and certification procedures. Since the "human potential" movement has been one of the fastest growing industries, with human growth centers dotting the continent from coast to coast and border to border, it has become necessary both to staff these installations as well as to meet the demand for intensive group experience in other settings. There simply are not enough persons available who could fulfill the criteria for certification as psychotherapists. And the groups, after all, must meet the growing demand.

Another limitation, although more subtle, imposed by the word "psychotherapy" is the implication that the therapist has the prime responsibility for either educating or moralizing the client. This implication violates the very foundation of the humanistic ethic as described by Bugental (1971): "each person is the *most responsible agency in his own life. . . .*" Thus, by using terms such as "leader" or "trainer" rather than therapist, the human growth experts have attempted to avoid the issue of responsibility. This issue has, nonetheless, been raised, especially following "casualties" or emotional breakdowns as a result of group participation. Even *The Village Voice* in 1969 raised the issue of responsibility when it refused to advertise groups whose claims *imply* therapy. Back (1972) describes the controversy:

> The paper said that advertising therapy was against professional standards and, in general, unethical. The sponsors of encounters argued that they did not conduct therapy or aim at changing the psychological state of participants in a fundamental way; a committee of encounter-group leaders said they aimed only "to provide a *social environment* for people who prefer not to relate to others in the distracting and sometimes artificial environments of bars, parties, dances, etc." (p. 31)

Regardless of how the humanistic group leaders choose to perceive their activities (e.g., as nontherapeutic alternatives to dance halls), and the names they give these activities (e.g., basic encounter groups, marathon growth sessions, human potential expanders, sensory awareness seminars), when they advertise their activities with the promise of "joy," "more joy," "peak joy," "cosmic joy," and even "advanced cosmic joy" they are bound to attract lonely, confused, distressed people. The humanists argue, quite convincingly, that the targets of these self-actualizing activities are not any of the "crazies" or "groupies" who often participate but rather more highly developed people, capable of realizing their full human potential following their intensive group experience. Indeed, the psychology of "ecstasy" and "rapture" is reserved for those who can afford the time, effort, and money to pursue metamotives and fulfill metaneeds.

There are, however, a number of humanists who call their activities "therapy." Because their approach runs counter to most psychotherapies, they have been accused of being less scientific, rigorous, and respectable. The focus of these therapies is on the body rather than the psyche. Keen (1970), a proponent of somatic therapy, explains:

They aim at the creation of a new man—sensuous, immediate, playful—whose prime vocation will be enjoyment, not labor ... Thus they define the task of therapy as awakening the senses and returning erotic awareness to the total body ... Their goal is greater wonder and sensitivity rather than more rationality and control. "Lose your mind and come to your senses," said Fritz Perls. (p. 56)

In order to accomplish these tasks, "the new therapeutic makes more use of *silence* than gab, of *sensation* than analysis, of phenomenological *observation* than theoretical explanation, of *touch* than 'therapeutic distance'" (Keen, 1970; italics ours). The formula, then, to create a new person is simply silence, sensation, observation, and touch. And what kind of a new person? One who is sensuous, immediate, and playful; who has lost his mind in order to come to his senses.

One can imagine Skinner's reaction to these goals and techniques. His probable disdain and disgust would have little relationship to the scientific merit of "humanistic" somatic therapy, but would no doubt be an expression of hostility toward the perverse, socially destructive value premises the goals and technique seem to reflect.

Again, rather than attempting to provide solutions for people with problems generated by living in inhumane situations, the "humanists" have distorted and coarsened even the meaning of their movement. Their verbal statements are, here too, nothing more than a "swollen word-string ... of the staple existential 'goodies'" (Koch, 1971). Their techniques neglect the intellectual, reflective, abstract elements of man.

In short, humanistic therapeutic techniques and nontherapeutic ones, like its theory, are little more than reflexive reaction against psychoanalysis and behaviorism. It is a distortion created by anti-intellectualism, by valuing silence over the exchange of ideas and information, and sensation over analysis. Humanism not only appears to have failed to provide a meaningful alternative to a revolt against "means-centeredness," but has combined with the other dehumanizing conceptions of man to produce new techniques with better camouflage for promoting a value-laden, quasireligious enterprise.

Other Voices, Other Rooms

A group of young, shrewd psychotherapists has responded to the exploitative, religious, and political nature of therapeutic encounters. Aware of the social control and manipulative aspects of psychotherapy, they reject the *present direction* of the control rather than the control itself. Forming a group known as "Radical Therapists," they claim that present-day psychotherapy, instead of serving people, perpetuates and legitimizes oppression. Glenn (1971), a spokesman for this position states:

Therapists by training, what we have been taught is increasingly irrelevant, and even destructive. Our notions of therapy are obsolete: elitist, male-centered, and obsessional. Our modes of practice are often racist and exploitative . . . we insulate ourselves from the society around us and support the status quo. (p. xv)

How do the radical therapists view therapy? To them, "therapy means political change . . . not peanut butter." In an editorial (in Agel, 1971) that responds to the question, "What is radical therapy?" First it emphasizes what it is not—it is not another *kind* of therapy, but rather a life-style; it is not what the therapist does, but how she/he lives and is. More specifically:

Radical therapy is any one of the following: organizing a community to *seize control* of the way it's run; helping a brother or sister through a crisis; rooting out our own chauvinism and mercilessly exposing it in others; focusing on the social dimensions of oppression and not on "intrapsychic" depression, fear, anger, and so on; organizing against the war, against polluting industries, against racist practice; developing a political/therapy center for young people . . . (p. 290)

This diverse range of activities is based, of course, upon several "illuminating" principles, which Steiner (1971) has expressed in terms of the following formulae:

Oppression + Deception = Alienation
Oppression + Awareness = Anger
Liberation = Awareness + Contact (Basic Radical Therapy
    Formula)

Since *contact* is an essential ingredient of liberation, radical therapy is best practiced in groups. They emphasize that awareness alone or contact alone cannot produce liberation. Thus, insight therapies (awareness) and encounter groups (contact) still leave people oppressed.

Although their position hardly needs further explication, a few words from another of the radical therapy theorists presents clearly the political foundation of their movement:

> Radical therapists must develop a theory of man and practice of therapy while integrating these into priorities and praxis for revolution. Only a radical therapy based on the Marxist *Weltanschauung* can accomplish all these tasks (Kupers, 1971, p. 44).

Thus, the poor, troubled, and distressed of the world are presented with another exploitative alternative: oppression by Marxism. Functionally, there is little difference between emptying man of freedom, dignity, autonomy, and intention, and filling man with oppression, anger, and hate in order to empty institutions and society of freedom. Both positions exploit the persons who they purport to help by placing more value on their ideologies than their patients. The radical therapist, when confronted with a person seeking help, serves that person by sending him out into society to struggle with the Establishment and to seize control of communities. The intention is to establish a new *status quo,* with new leaders coming, undoubtedly, from the ranks of the radical therapists. Unlike the behaviorists and humanists who are content with the present state of affairs, the radical therapists want to establish a new social structure where they (and the people, of course) control all the variables. The radical therapists, with their slogans and political clichés make no attempt to hide behind "science"; instead, they are out front, facilitating our task here of drawing the relationship of psychotherapy to social, political, and economic forces.

The therapies we discussed are not alone with respect to the intertwining of values and therapeutic goals and practices. For instance, Ellis (1967) maintains that the therapist *should* act as a propagandist, primarily for the mainstream values. Freud (1927) described the functional role of the analyst as "a secular spiritual guide." London (1964) in an astute analysis of "the secular priesthood," remarks:

> Life would be easier for psychotherapists if they were able to contain their role entirely within the bounds of something called "breakdown" . . . The concept of therapeutic repair of breakdown is essentially retrospective and as such is fairly amenable to concrete description and solution. But the problem of concern here is prospective, concerning a future that is always vague, and that is therefore hard to address wisely . . . problems of *salvation* . . . Once psychotherapists choose to address such behaviors, they implicitly choose thereby to arbitrate and mediate those [moral] codes. How? By what schemes? According to what values? (pp. 160–161)

Although London feels that there is nothing outwardly wrong with psychotherapists attempting to fill the moral vacuum in the lives of modern men, we find much wrong with it. Indeed, throughout this book we have indicated repeatedly how the morality and value premises of psychologists have obfuscated and distorted the human condition. The ramifications in the research enterprise are less disconcerting than the outcomes of such misconstructions when psychologists deal directly with people in the diagnostic and therapeutic enterprises.

The alternatives psychology has provided to institutionalized mental patients, incarcerated children, the misfits, and surplus populations speaks poorly, indeed, of the theories, research practices, and conceptions of man proclaimed by the profession.

EIGHT

Psychology Tomorrow

We have, thus far, examined today's mainstream movements in American psychology from the perspectives of their formal theories, research activities, and clinical practices, as well as the extrascientific areas that have influenced each realm. The record of the psychological enterprise is replete with inconsistencies, ideological dogma, vast regions of ignorance, unenlightening jargon, and questionable activities and practices. At a time when people need new knowledge about the human situation, we find most psychologists, although they appear to be making "discoveries," unwitting but effective social apologists. Were it not for the serious ramifications of psychology's failures, the history of mainstream psychology would be more suitable as a chapter in *Catch-22* than as subject matter for the *Encyclopaedia Britannica*.

There are several reasons why the failure of the psychological enterprise is a serious matter. Psychologists, unlike other social scientists, interface with the public on many levels and, as authorities on human behavior, have the potential to adversely affect ordinary citizens. When a sociologist, for instance, distorts social reality by using meaningless jargon and produces measurements to substantiate his illogical concept, rarely does anyone directly suffer. He may err in the confines of academe, yet still be praised by his colleagues and emulated by graduate students. Fortunately, the ordinary citizen usually will not be affected by his errors.

If, on the other hand, a psychologist in academe makes logical errors and produces absurdities, "applied" psychologists will, nonetheless, use the "scientific" material in schools, industry, mental institutions, and the community. Psychology has, in fact, become such a formidable influence in our society that the ordinary citizen is affected by it from infancy to old age. Child-rearing manuals written by child psychology experts (or others who use their research discoveries) prepare the parents to "handle" their child in his formative years. Upon entering school, the child is confronted with teachers who have been guided by experts in educational psychology. As soon as the child is able to read and write, he is given tests developed by psychological experts to measure human capacities, especially intelligence. The scores the child obtains, to a large extent, determine his educational and, therefore, his occupational career. The child, as a young man, will apply for a job. It is very likely that psychologists will intrude into this man's life with aptitude and personality tests, and, if the position sought is a high-level one, perhaps a stress interview. Let us assume he is hired and, after a few years, is in a middle management position. He may find his work interrupted by industrial psychology experts who have convinced the president of the company that they can improve management performance with their specially developed group training techniques. Later, the man may desire a change of career and may turn for assistance to a counseling psychologist. He also may feel that his marriage should be terminated but might be advised to first seek the help of a marriage counseling psychologist or, since there are children involved, a family psychotherapist.

Thus, the ordinary citizen at many significant points in his life is confronted with psychological experts who have an inordinate and undeserved amount of power in determining his future. Should the citizen at any time in his otherwise average life engage in behaviors that are interpreted as deviant, the power of the psychologists increases dramatically.

We cannot stress enough the inadvertent nature of most psychologists' participation in this potentially destructive enterprise. Most psychologists, particularly those who deal directly with people, have the best of intentions and sincerely desire to help the individual. They are merely misguided by the psychological principles and procedures they were trained to value over, perhaps, their own better judgment. For instance, quantification and measurement have become in and of themselves guidelines for the psychological enterprise. This dependence upon numbers and scores, old as psychology itself, presents some serious dangers, not only in the laboratory, but especially when applied to human attributes. Over 25 years ago, Köhler (1947) anticipated the legal action recently brought against the California State Board of Education when he discussed IQ scores in just this context:

> The scores are mere numbers which allow of many different interpretations . . . a given score may mean: degree 3 of "intelligence," together with degree 1 of "accuracy," with degree 4 of "ambition" and degree 3 of "quickness of fatigue." But it may also mean "intelligence" 6, "accuracy" 2, "ambition" 1 and "quickness of fatigue" 4 . . . Thus combinations of certain components in varying proportions may give precisely the same I.Q. . . . a child ought to be treated according to the nature and strength of the specific factors which co-operate in establishing his total I.Q. . . . *We are still much too easily satisfied by our tests because, as quantitative procedures, they look so pleasantly scientific.* (p. 45; italics ours)

Thus, psychologists will try, at almost all costs, to maintain their appearance as scientists. Their preoccupation with the various technologies of science, noted earlier in the book, has once again returned. It is this highly valued role that renders psychologists vulnerable to extrascientific influences. In their desire to become scientists, psychologists have acted like the proverbial drunkard who, though he lost his keys in a dark alley, searches for them a half block away under the street lamp because it's lighter there and easier to see.

The failure of mainstream psychology is apparent since numerous psychologists have attempted to draw our attention to that dark alley. It is not, therefore, for want of alternative perspectives that most psychologists have followed behaviorist or humanist ideas. Instead, as we indicated earlier, these movements became representative of the mainstream because they so closely parallel the two dominant socio-political-religious positions in American society. Graduate students and new psychologists, drawn like most people to that which is familiar and educated in the translation of their socio-political-religious ideologies into science, are encouraged and rewarded for staying under the street lamp.

Evidence has been compiled that shows exactly how well the psychological enterprise holds its own despite deviant positions within the profession. In a recent nationwide survey of graduate students and faculty in psychology (NISP Tech. Report #15, APA, 1970), over 2000 students responded to the item, "Which one person in psychology or a related area has produced the work you most respect?" Skinner outpolled all psychologists with 10 percent of the students mentioning him; Rogers and Freud followed each with 4 percent; and 3 percent for Piaget. Over 350 faculty members responded similarly with 11 percent for Skinner, 8 percent for Neal Miller, and 2 percent each for Piaget, Hebb, and Lewin. By far, the psychologist who presented the most simplistic ideological position was the most popular. Least likely to be included were those who have appealed to:

> . . . a disposition to deal with the facts rather than what someone has said about them . . . a willingness to accept facts even when they are opposed to wishes . . . intellectual honesty . . . refrain from making statements on insufficient evidence . . . avoid explanations which are pure invention . . . (Skinner, 1953, pp. 12–13)

What, then, have the deviants in the psychological enterprise had to contribute in the way of alternatives to the dominant movements? Before we proceed, however, it should be noted that one thing they do not provide is a "movement," nor do they seek to attract "true believers" to their cause. Hoffer (1951) in his description of the appeal a doctrine has to true believers indicates how movements are antithetical to the pursuit of knowledge:

> They depict an autonomous, self-sufficient existence not only as barren and meaningless but also as depraved and evil. Man on his own is a helpless, miserable and sinful creature. His only salvation is in rejecting his self and in finding a new life in the bosom of a holy corporate body . . . (p. 55)

Thus, the less popular viewpoints of psychology appeal to man-as-scientist. They present no world view, no heaven, no ritual, nor any other anxiety reducing mechanisms. They do provide, however, uncertainty rather than certainty, questions rather than answers, and adventure rather than complacency—surely not an alternative for the meek or mediocre.

Students, who are preparing for this venture while still in the midst of mainstream psychology, are faced with a difficult task. They must not only be able to distinguish between the sense and nonsense of psychology but also to immunize themselves against the ideological thrusts of its theories, research, and practices. Hopefully, this book will help in these discrimination tasks. The following brief guidelines may facilitate evaluation.

This test is keyed so that the larger the number of "yes" responses the poorer the score for the theory, research, or practice in question.

1. *Is the observed behavior "caused" by some inner mechanism, structure, or process?* (Or is it "caused" by outer mechanisms, structures, or processes? For example, a child's crying may be caused by id impulses, chromosomal combinations, habit strength, cybernetic feedback, neurological connections, or because the wall he bumped into punished him.)
2. *Are these inner or outer mechanisms, structures, or processes defined solely by the operations of the psychologist?* (For example, intelligence defined by an IQ test score; emotional

development by TAT cards; drive strength by hours of deprivation.)

3. *Is it possible to disprove the existence of these mechanisms, structures, or processes?* (A hypothetical construct by definition is a fiction, and a fiction by definition cannot be proved or disproved since it does not exist. Thus one cannot disprove the existence of repression, drive reduction, conditioning, reinforcement, or ego-strength anymore than one can disprove the existence of a rain god.)

4. *Are the behaviors "caused" by these mechanisms, structures, or processes independent of the social context in which they occur and the awareness of the behaving organism?* (In other words, the clenched fist is raised in anger? greeting? muscle stretching? involuntary reflex?)

5. *Does the psychologist create the environment in which these mechanisms cause particular behaviors?* (That is, are the settings used to study behavior real-life [e.g., classroom], simulations of real life [e.g., the room a subject is *led to believe* is a classroom] or the private world of the psychologist [*t* maze]?)

6. *Are the behaviors "caused" by these mechanisms best (or only) seen in a psychologist-created environment?* (For example, how often do people jump off electric grids to avoid shocks, or tell stories about inkblots?)

7. *Can the mechanisms, structures, or processes be seen as "good" or "bad" for the organism?* (Although this is not a critical point, it can sensitize the student to the implicit ideology. For instance, id = bad, ego = good; memory = good, forgetting = bad; conformity = bad, autonomy = good.)

8. *Does the language confuse?* (For example, is one word or concept used to explain everything from bar pressing to the evolution of cultures [i.e., reinforcement contingencies] or does a new word appear every sentence [see Cattell, Murray, Maslow to name a few]? Is familiar language used in peculiar ways? For instance, defining the withholding of food from a hungry man until the man emits the desired behavior as positive reinforcement.)

We are sure concerned students can expand this test. Other criteria can and should be generated by those who are concerned about the future of psychology.

The Other Psychology

In our critique of the humanist and behaviorist movements in psychology, we focused upon their manifestations in the clinical and experimental enterprise. The roots of these movements were, in fact, in these two specialty areas (for behaviorism, experimental psychology; and for humanism, clinical psychology), although they have been transported in varying degrees to other areas of psychology (social, developmental, industrial, school, pastoral, philosophical, etc.). The extent to which these areas have incorporated the mainstream ideologies into their fields is reflected in the failures and absurdities of their productions. The industrial psychologist, for instance, who sees himself as a behaviorist will be just as misguided as the behavioristic experimental psychologist and the clinician with his faradic aversive conditioning apparatus.

Social psychology has been less amenable than the other specialty areas in psychology to the influence of behavioristic or humanistic ideologies and has, consequently, escaped much of the absurdities, destructiveness, and failures of both. The relative impermeability of its boundaries is related, in part, to the historical development and intellectual tradition of social psychology. This does not mean that social psychology does not include behaviorists or humanists, or that it has not produced its own volumes of irrelevant research. Indeed, Kenneth Ring (1967), in a brilliant analysis, assails the "fun-and-games approach" to research in social psychology where "flamboyance" rather than significance is dictating more and more the selection of research topics and research design.

Despite many shortcomings and excursions into the mainstream, social psychology represents the one area in the psychological enterprise that has through the years produced theory and research relevant to the human situation and human experience. Social psychologists have searched areas that have been unsanctioned for centuries; topics not only unresearched but rarely mentioned in public—authoritarianism, conformity, obedience, brain-washing, ingratiation, manipulation. They have, at times, ventured in their research activities outside of the laboratories into actual settings with ordinary people. But perhaps most important, they have recognized that there can be no understanding of the human situation unless human experience is an integral part of the social psychological enterprise.

> Every field of inquiry must begin with the phenomena that everyday experience reveals, and with the distinctions it contains. Further inquiry may modify our understanding of them, but the phenomena themselves will never be displaced. (Asch, 1959, p. 379)

At its inception, one of the major concerns of psychology was, in fact, human experience. The introspectionists, among the first formal "schools" of psychology, maintained that descriptions could give us a science of direct experience. They discredited, however, the importance of human experience by timidly focusing their attention on peripheral trifles and descriptions of minute experiences (e.g., pin pricks, pressed eyeballs). As Köhler (1947) noted, "Apparently they have agreed upon facing important problems as seldom as possible, and to occupy themselves mainly with nuances in the field of sensation." Although introspection has long been abandoned, every field of inquiry in psychology, including behaviorism, begins with the phenomena of everyday experience. These phenomena, however, are soon renounced once the theorizing begins and research is underway.

Concerned about the abandonment of human experience in psychology, Asch (1952) wrote:

> Modern psychology has often drawn, I suspect, a caricature rather than a portrait of man. As a result it has introduced a grave gap between itself and *the knowledge of man that observation gives us* and *from which investigation must start.* Those who are not psychologists (and psychologists when they are off duty) speak of such strange things as fair play, justice and injustice, even of dignity and the need for freedom. They act on the asumption that men are the kind of beings that have the capacity to understand, that they have a sense of responsibility and can distinguish

right from wrong . . . Yet not only are these ideas excluded from scientific discusion; the conceptual schemes with which psychology works today hardly leave room for them . . . Is it possible, however, that psychological ideas can be adequate which neglect aspects as important as those we have mentioned? We have a right to wonder whether this is not a *spurious objectivity,* whether it does not have its roots in a certain decadence and *anti-human orientation* for which the subject matter itself is not responsible, and whether *the simplicity and apparent freedom from presuppositions may* not *hide a dogmatism all the more inflexible because it speaks in the name of science.* (pp. 24–25; italics ours)

As our earlier analysis of mainstream psychology indicated, the "apparent freedom from presuppositions," does, indeed, hide a dogmatism that severely hampers the search for knowledge. Mainstream psychology first judges, theorizes, and manipulates and, then, proceeds to "look" at the subject matter. To no one's surprise, it often "finds" exactly what it expected. Fairminded observation and nonbiased searching, a rare occurrence in the psychological enterprise, is not enough, however, for psychology to free itself from its distortions. Psychology must first shed much of what it has called its own as well as incorporate areas that, in the past, it ignored.

For instance, Barker (1968), a social psychologist who, for years, has been studying the actual environment in which behavior occurs, is chagrined by psychology's failure to study the human environment:

The descriptive, natural history, ecological phase of investigation has had a minor place in psychology, and this has seriously limited the science . . . One might think that psychology would have become informed about the fundamental nature of the ecological environment in the course of its study of the context of behavior. But this is not the case . . . psychology has attended almost exclusively to those elements of the environment that are useful in probing the behavior-relevant circuitry within the skins of its subjects . . . in accordance with the *principles of experimental design it has excised these environmental elements from the complexities of the real-life settings* in which they occur . . .

The result is, inevitably, that *the science of psychology has no adequate knowledge of the psychologist-free environment of behavior.* (pp. 1, 4; italics ours)

In a later paper, Barker (1969) admonishes mainstream psychology for having nothing to contribute, despite millions of man hours and dollars spent on research, to the increasingly urgent social problems that confront man:

What are the consequences for human behavior of such environmental conditions as poverty . . . congested cities, transient populations, high population density, computer technology, ghettoes, large schools, "bedroom" communities? . . . The present method, concepts, and theories of the psychological sciences cannot answer the new questions . . . Scientific psychology knowns nothing, and can know nothing, about the real-life settings in which people live, in ghettoes and suburbs, in large and small schools, in regions of poverty and affluence . . . Its prevailing methods of research shatter whatever pattern and organization may exist within the natural environment. (p. 36)

The solution Barker (1969) quietly proposes is nothing short of a conceptual revolution in mainstream psychology. Specifically, the task of the investigator based simply on fair-minded, unbiased observations "is *to translate phenomena* and their descriptions *without alteration* into the language of data" (italics ours). In their best form, Barker (1969) continues, *"ecological data* are *phenomena-centered* and they are *atheoretical"* (italics ours). Thus, Barker suggests that psychologists not only venture forth from their carefully controlled laboratories into a chaotic environment, but also that they leave behind their theories, their preconceptions, and their linguistic accessories. It is no surprise that Barker has neither won any popularity poll among psychologists nor generated a great deal of research activity employing his ecological principles.

A number of psychologists have, however, ventured into the real world as participant observers and have produced some of the most valuable and exciting research reports in psychology. Festinger, Riecken, and Schachter (1956), for example, studied a group movement whose leader prophesied the destruction of the world. More recently, the participant observer technique has been employed with dramatic results by Rosenhan (1973) in the role of a mental patient in a variety of institutional settings. Both studies involved deceptions concerning the identity of the investigators in order to create or maintain a "psychologist-free" environment.

There are other field research possibilities available to the investigator who is either faint-of-heart or totally unable to dissimulate (the latter would exclude the possibility of conducting even laboratory studies requiring manipulations and keeping the subjects naïve by omissive lies). For instance, Latané and Darley (1968, 1969) have, by creating real-life situations, explored the phenomena of bystander apathy when another person is in distress. Some researchers have merely observed on-going group activities in their natural setting using schema such as those proposed by Barker (1968), Bales (1950), and others. Still other research psychologists have gone to actual settings and have tried to ascertain the psychological ecology and experience of those who live in those settings (Braginsky, Braginsky, & Ring, 1969; Braginsky & Braginsky, 1971).

The point, here, is that numerous research strategies are available to those who choose to conduct their investigations in places other than the laboratory. Moreover, there are strategies at hand that could make even laboratory studies more meaningful. Psychology must free itself from two detrimental myths: (1) that discrete, observable behaviors are the only data for psychological studies; and (2) that these behaviors must be emitted (or elicited) in a highly controlled, artificial environment created by the experimenter. Psychologists would then no longer be oppressed by and burdened with all the corollary pretensions and anxieties. In particular, their xenophobic fears, hopefully put to rest, would not foist esoteric, meaningless, and boring problems upon them. This anxiety, Homans (1967) points out, has been detrimental to the progress of psychology:

In studying human behavior social scientists are studying phenomena that human beings are uniquely familiar with. As social animals, nothing has been more important to them, and there is nothing they have learned more about. Since they are also talking animals and can pass on their knowledge, the knowledge has been accumulating for hundreds of thousands of years. (p. 53)

As a result of this age-old activity, Homans (1967) notes that the ordinary person not only knows the principles of behavioral psychology but acts on them and uses them to plan his own behavior. Social scientists have responded to this familiarity with contempt, which has only hampered the scientific enterprise. The principles and fundamental propositions, according to Homans (1967):

. . . seem so obvious as to be boring, and an intellectual, by definition a wit and a man of the world, will go to any mad lengths to avoid the obvious. Add to this the dilemma created by the assumption that making fundamental discoveries is the mark of a science . . . The most significant difference between social science and other sciences is that *its principles do not have to be discovered but,* what is more difficult, *simply recognized for what they are.* (p. 53; italics ours)

How do we come to know these principles and to recognize these fundamental propositions? Lewin, the single most influential theorist in social psychology, suggested over 50 years ago that, "An investigator need only go where the work is, *look, listen,* and *record*" (Marrow, 1969; italics ours). As his investigations progressed and his field theory crystallized, in the 1920's Lewin (1935, 1936) introduced the formula $B = f (p, e)$, a formula that was to be so widely adopted in social psychology that it appeared to be intrinsic to the area itself.

Very simply, Lewin's field theory postulates that behavior (B) is a function of the person (p) and the environment (e), and that both the person and the environment are interdependent variables. That is, they are not separate or separable entities but, instead, coexist within a dynamic field. Thus, all behavior, including thinking, desiring, or striving, is a product of this dynamic field of interdependent variables—the *life space.* According to Lewin (1935), the "life space is the total psychological environment which the person experiences subjectively."

The life space, composed of everything existing for the person in a given unit of time (needs, goals, memories, aspirations, political or social events, fear, unconscious forces, etc.), is where we may go to understand, analyze, and illuminate further the ancient discoveries of man.

The experimentalist and the clinician, for different reasons, may be wary of such a "subjective" phenomenological approach and skeptical that any good could ever come of it. Let us, therefore, utilize this approach on one problem that has plagued mainstream psychology for nearly 100 years: learning. The illustrations described are didactic, representing available possibilities rather than *the* alternative to mainstream psychology.

The Other Psychology of "Learning"

The topic of learning has received more attention than, perhaps, any other in mainstream psychology. It has generated numerous theories, voluminous amounts of research, and a wide variety of practical applications. Experimental psychologists, physiological psychologists, clinical psychologists, educational psychologists, and even some social psychologists have spent lifetimes investigating learning. Indeed, it is seen by many psychologists as the key to understanding (and, of course, controlling) all behavior. They reason that since all behavior is learned (except perhaps spinal reflexes), and since learning occurs when the organism is in contact with the physical and social environment, delineating the processes or the environmental factors involved in learning will possibly enable psychologists to control almost every aspect of behavior.

This vague hope has allowed psychologists to study bar-pressing behavior of rats, spinal reflexes of cats, the neural pathways of rhesus monkeys, nonsense syllable retention of college sophomores, and maze running of gerbils, to mention just a few, while searching for the key to learning. Only then can the real problems of man be solved—problems ranging from why Johnny can't learn how to read, to why Myra can't learn to be a better wife, to why nations can't learn to cooperate and live peacefully with each other.

Despite all the time and effort psychologists have devoted to studying learning, all this research has not yielded any knowledge that can teach us anything about learning. After 100 years of rigorous and vigorous effort, Johnny still can't learn to read—in fact, more Johnnys than ever cannot learn to read. What, then, is this concept that psychologists call learning? Why haven't they found out more about it?

There is, to date, no acceptable, unambiguous, meaningful definition of learning in psychology. Most attempted definitions, in fact, cannot conceptually distinguish learning from memory. Be that as it may, most psychologists would, in their effort to show what learning is, refer to the phenomena that behavior is shaped through contact with the environment. Although this still tells us nothing about learning, it points to an incontrovertible *fact*. If an organism, after exposure to a situation, elicits a response that he could not (or did not) exhibit prior to that exposure, something surely has occurred. That "something" is called "learning." Moreover, further evidence that "something" has occurred has been produced by physiological psychologists who have recorded neurological changes during learning. Even though they are unclear about the nature of the psychological event called learning, they, as Chein (1972) puts it, "industriously speculate about the physiological conditions and concomitants of [these] psychological events." The correlation between the physiological and the unidentified psychological processes is used to defend the belief of many psychologists "that the psychic phenomena are nothing but physiological" (Chein, 1972). The faulty reasoning of the proponents of such a position, keenly analyzed by Chein (1972), is attributed to the failure of psychologists to discern that a correlation "cannot establish identity, not even if the correlation is unity." Chein (1972) contends further that "no amount of observation of physiological process can demonstrate anything but physiological process and . . . it cannot do so because there is nothing there but physiological process."

The psychologist interested in learning does not have to rely on physiological data to convince people that learning is a *real* phenomena. We know from experience that learning occurs. As adults, we are different than we were as children, and that difference is accounted for by what we have learned in those intervening years. Not only have we acquired knowledge from experiences, but we also recall having devoted much effort to trying to learn specific information, such as the alphabet, the rules of contract bridge, or driving a car. The direct phenomenological experience, then, is the basis for selecting learning as a topic for psychological inquiry. But can learning be treated as a topic separate from all other areas of psychology?

If we agree that learning is, very broadly, acquisition based upon experience or contact with the environment, then learning is synonomous with experience. So long as a person (and perhaps other organisms), sees, smells, touches, or hears, he is acquiring information about his environment. A man traveling in a crowded subway car may be learning a variety of things, ranging from the ethics of acquiring a seat to the variations in the sounds and smells around him.

Thus, if the psychology of learning kept its phenomenological basis, then logic would dictate a redefinition of the area. Psychologists would not define their field of interest as "learning," but, instead, would specify the content of the human experience in which they are interested. For example, a psychologist would define his particular area as the experience of verbal material, or the experience of physically coordinated activity, or the experience of other people. But psychologists interested in learning, particularly behaviorists, are explicitly antiphenomenological. Although they justify the importance of their endeavors by embedding the phenomena in conscious experience, they completely abandon it in their professional activities, using, instead, "scientific" operational definitions. We have already discussed the activity of defining concepts solely in terms of the experimenter's operations. Defining learning as the electrical activity of neurons, or the speed at which a rat completes a maze, or salivation at the sound of a bell, or the number of nonsense syllables a person reproduces is analogous to defining the moon by a dance we perform or a child by the kiss we plant on his cheek.

In summary, the psychology of learning is expressed in the

following illogical sequence: the phenomenological experience of acquiring and storing things is used as a basis to demarcate an area of investigation; this area is then redefined by theories and practices that deny entirely its origins, replacing them with the absurdity that learning is any kind of response that fits the operations of the researcher or theorist.

We are not denying that observable changes in behavior, including the acquisition of new behavior, occur after exposure to certain situations. Claudia and Craig, for instance, did not know how to ride a bicycle. After instruction, however, their bicycle riding markedly improved. We are not rejecting the observation that people change after experiencing something. Instead, we are asserting that since people are *always experiencing,* they are *always acquiring* and *always changing*—or, if you prefer, *always learning.*

At this point, the psychology experts in learning may be pleased, indeed, since they have contended all along that everything is a function of learning. However, the thrust of our critique would be misconstrued if they were to conclude that we propose to give psychology to the learning specialists. To the contrary, our argument would remove "learning" from the traditional learning theories and place it, instead, in the Lewinian formulation: $B = f(p, e)$. Learning, here, is the behavior, a function of the human situation, not a function of experimenter operations, shaping, or stimulus–response connections.

Thus, we need psychologists who can become experts in studying the life space, the human situation, and the transactions between people, not "learning" specialists who, by their own definitions, can only obscure and preclude the meaning of learning in human affairs.

How and where would a psychologist search for the processes that are assumed to underly the acquisition of knowledge and behavior change? The answer, here, is that the search for processes (whatever "processes" may mean) leads only to an obscured problem. To chase after processes assumed to inhabit the inner reaches of man or the outer reaches of the physical environment is a frantic and meaningless activity. This book, in fact, is replete with examples of the failures borne of such activities.

Instead, we might more fruitfully begin by entirely reformulating our questions. We all know, for example, that people *experience* learning. Learning is a word that is part of every person's vocabulary and is used to distinguish one kind of experience from another. Thus, we might ask: What is man's experience of learning? Under what conditions do most people agree that learning has taken place? When does a person experience success or failure with respect to learning? What are the criteria people use and how do these vary from group to group, or situation to situation?

Furthermore, if we are interested in how a person deals with and stores that which he has learned, we must determine whether the person is in a classroom, a burlesque show, a phone booth, a submarine, a bathroom, or a concentration camp. We will have to know how important he considers this acquisition, and to what area of his life does it have relevance (his job, his leisure, his family, his survival). In addition, we will have to inquire whether he intends to store and preserve the material for a few minutes, a few hours, or a lifetime. We might find it worthwhile to ascertain what he thinks about himself and his performance.

We must, in short, begin by asking questions that will allow us to construct man's experiences about learning rather than by creating our own operational constructions. Obviously, this approach cannot be applied to gerbils, white rats, monkeys, frogs, worms, or other organisms with whom we cannot communicate. It also implies that psychologists must overcome their aversion to questioning people, as well as their propensity to see people's answers as verbal responses (S–R circuitry, unconscious desires, etc.), representing anything but answers.

An almost infinite variety of possibilities arises from the phenomenological perspective of learning. Let us turn to a concrete situation, a student in school, and elaborate upon a few of these possibilities. In our hypothetical investigation we have spent many hours with a first-grade student mapping out his experience of the schoolroom and of learning. If the reader feels more comfortable with larger numbers of subjects, let us assume, further, that we have collated similar information about twenty students in that classroom. What kind of information might we obtain from studying the children's life space?

Foremost in our imaginary data, we find that the classroom is perceived as being different from other rooms in the children's lives. It is a large room occupied by a number of other children, most of whom originally are strangers to each other. The focal point of the classroom, the teacher, not only looks different than the other people in the room (she's bigger, older, stronger), but her desk is different and is situated apart from the students' desks. Indeed, the teacher *is,* for most of them, *the* situation. The children perceived themselves as a part of a homogeneous "background" group and the teacher as "figure."

On the basis of their hypothetical descriptions, it is evident that the experience of classroom is dramatically different than the experience of living room or rumpus room, and that upon entering the classroom the children become different as well. That is, moving from the world of a parent's child to that of a teacher's student socially transforms the children. A social transformation also occurs for the teacher, who makes a conscious effort to present an image to her students that is quite different from the one she maintains at her breakfast table.

Other factors contribute to the children's experience of the schoolroom, such as a long history of anticipations and, perhaps, anxiety. The children were aware that their parents saw the schoolroom as an important place for them to be, a place where they would change for the better, a place where they would "learn" valued things, such as reading and writing. They knew, even before many could understand, that special things would be offered to them that they could not get elsewhere. Within a very short time, however, the children became aware of what "learning" meant and what it was they were supposed to learn.

As they might have described it, the learning situation means that the teacher has things inside of her to give them. She has, for example, a way of taking letters and making them into words. When they can do the same things the teacher does, they have "learned." Later, they reported that they experienced learning, not only when they could do what the teacher did, but when they felt sure that they could store it for long periods of time as well. If they could not preserve the material, they experienced "forgetting," which, to them, was almost as bad as not learning, since the teacher disapproved of both.

With the first-graders' phenomenological experience of learning as background, let us look again at the term "learning." The previous simple analysis strongly suggests the existence of a special kind of social transaction not unlike that which occurs in economic situations. This exchange, however, is between the children's "proper behavior" and the teacher's approval. From this new vantage point, learning is not some intrapsychic occurrence in the child, nor the manipulations the teacher performs. Instead, it appears that learning is a special outcome of a particular kind of transaction between significantly different people. The special outcome is one person's public behavior that matches another person's criteria for a proper ("learned") performance. Learning refers, then, to a relationship, not to invisible internal processes or environmental forces.

The children's reports of their experience of learning in school provided further insights in this area. They might have told us, for instance, that some kinds of learning are more valuable than other kinds, and that the teacher gives more praise for some acquisitions than for others. The general rule they recognized to determine the worth of any acquisition is the less people who are able to acquire it, or the more people who fail to learn it, the more valuable it is. Thus, the children value the esoteric, abstruse aspects of learning more than the self-evident knowledge that most people can acquire easily.

Traditionally, learning despite the "hidden" criteria for a proper performance, has been assumed to be a function of some abstract capacity. For example, most young children know the words "cow" and "man," yet they find it difficult to include both "cow" and "man" in one category called "animal." The category "animal' is seen as a higher order, more abstract concept than either "man" or "cow." That is, the category "animal" is not simply dependent upon concrete perceptual information easily acquired through direct experience. The child, therefore, in order to perform properly, must acquire a new premise concerning the nature of the world in which he lives. Since this premise does not exist in his direct experience, it must be given to him by others. Thus, the concept of *abstract capacity* does not refer to some putative higher order conceptual process. Instead, it tells us that the criteria chosen for proper performance is based on a vague premise, and that it can only be acquired by contact with others.

A phenomenological perspective enables us to see what learning is to most people and to outline the relevant parameters of this activity so that we might intelligently move beyond this level of analysis. Further, we can also ascertain what it is that people learn by simply asking them. This issue is a controversial one among learning theorists, with some contending that it is cognitive maps that are learned, others "stimulus–response chains," and still others "contingencies of reinforcement."

Asch (1959) illustrated the problems encountered by researchers who neglect phenomenological data by citing one of Skinner's (1953) prescriptions for a psychological utopia. Skinner proposed a procedure to train children to tolerate frustration, which consists of occasionally delaying their meals for a few minutes while they look at the delicious foods that were prepared for them. The period of deprivation would gradually be extended to instill more and more self-control without injurious consequences. On the basis of Skinner's description, the procedure appears to be exclusively a matter of timed responses to given physical conditions. Asch (1959) notes, however, that the children may have a very different view of Skinner's procedure:

> Are they not likely to *wonder* what their caretakers are up to? . . . If it should *come into the children's heads* that the caretakers are malicious, it might go ill with the effects of the scheduling. On the other hand, if the children *trusted* their mentors . . . the discipline might prove more successful. (p. 376; italics ours)

Thus, the denial of experience, wondering, thinking, and trusting in this illustration amounts to a conceptual and descriptive failure as well as a moral one.

If we examine the typical psychological learning experiment, it is strikingly similar to the schoolroom. The experimenter, like the teacher, has particular criteria for correct performance by the subjects (students). If the criteria are met, the subject has "learned" the material. Unlike the teacher, however, the psychologist keeps his subjects naïve, never divulging to them what he is looking for or what principle of "learning" he is testing. Indeed, one major component of the traditional learning experiment, although not taken into consideration, is the subject's attempts to guess the experimenter's "secret" for proper performance. It is not surprising that college students are good subjects, since most of their lives have been spent acquiring the rules of proper performance. What is startling is the relative ease with which white rats can successfully meet the experimenter's arbitrary, hidden criteria.

Many of the controversies between the learning theorists (indeed the learning theories, themselves) would dissolve if we would look again at the observations that gave rise to the confusion. The observation, for instance, of rapidly declining retention curves for information subjects "learned" using memory drum techniques had led to a variety of psychological explanations. Decaying memory traces, weakened stimulus–response associations, and lack of reinforcement, among other notions, have been posited to explain the subjects' rapid forgetting. One explanation that has not been entertained is, perhaps, that the subject's desire to rid themselves of the nonsense syllables they "learned," and to expend no more time and energy trying to retain that material. That is, the rapidly declining *retention* rates are not indexes of any principle of learning but are, more likely, graphic representations of people's response to trivia and trivial situations—they forget them as soon as possible.

In summary, a phenomenological analysis of "learning" can provide a multiple of potentially rich avenues of exploration. Our brief analysis was not intended to represent a systematic, formal, or detailed inquiry, but rather to illustrate one major point: when old "sets" are broken and shed, exciting alteratives for research psychologists abound. Reality speaks loudly once we drop ideological preconceptions, filling the void of the discarded answers with numerous fascinating, important questions. We know now, for example, that people use the term "learn" in many different contexts (e.g., I "learned" how to ski; I "learned" what he really was like; I "learned" to keep my mouth shut; I "learned" what it's like to be sick), and that it is not unscientific or deplorable to explore these meanings and contexts. If we maintain the old strategies of research, these avenues of diverse and rich information about people and situations will never be open to us.

Psychology Now

We have tried, in this final chapter, to indicate that it is not only possible for psychology to function outside of the mainstream movement, but that it is the only way we can begin to explore and to understand the human situation. Although we know that psychologists, like most people, have value premises, stereotypes, and preconceptions, we also are aware that they do not have to be the servants of their ideology. We do not propose that psychologists assume a detached, disinterested, amoral posture, but instead that they recognize and make public their ideology, as well as its potential impact on their work. Many psychologists have shown that values and moral commitments do not have to interfere with well-planned theories, fairminded observations in research activities, or honest, open relationships in clinical practices.

Psychologists do not have to assume ridiculous, pseudo-scientific postures, or use jargonized language in order to distinguish themselves from other people. Psychologists have already been recognized for their differences by the public, which has commissioned them to help people understand and improve the human condition. Removing the myths about psychologists' roles would place them firmly in the realm of public accountability and responsibility.

Psychologists do not have to work for society or any single group in order to justify their existence. In serving the powerful, psychologists have violated their contract with the ordinary citizen. This does not mean that psychologists should not become involved with intervention or social action. Rather, the intervention must be based upon knowledge of the human situation, not what we believe or wish it to be. The unwitting intrusions of ideology and false assumptions account, no doubt, for the failures of many well-intentioned and desperately needed social action programs. In short, we are not suggesting that psychologists not act, but when they do, to act fairly and intelligently.

Many psychologists, from William James to Alfred Adler to Kurt Lewin (and his myriad of productive students), have pointed the way. The discontent in psychology is evident, and change, we hope, is near. Perhaps we may soon begin to explore the terrain that drew so many of us into psychology and that so enchanted us.

References

Adorno, T. W., Frenkel-Brunswik, E., Levinson, D. J., & Sanford, R. N. *The Authoritarian Personality.* New York: Harper & Row, 1950.

Agel, J. (Prod.). *The Radical Therapist.* New York: Ballantine, 1971.

Allport, G. W. *Becoming.* New Haven: Yale University Press, 1955.

American Psychiatric Association. *Diagnostic and Statistical Manual of Mental Disorders.* Washington, D.C.: 1952.

Anderson, Barry F. *The Psychology Experiment: An Introduction to Scientific Method.* Belmont, Calif.: Brooks/Cole, 1971.

Asch, S. E. *Social Psychology.* Englewood Cliffs, N.J.: Prentice-Hall, 1952.

Asch, S. E. A perspective on social psychology. In S. Koch (Ed.), *Psychology: A Study of a Science.* Vol. 3. New York: McGraw-Hill, 1959.

Ash, P. The reliability of psychiatric diagnosis. *Journal of Abnormal and Social Psychology,* 1949, *44,* 272–276.

Ayllon, T. Intensive treatment of psychotic behavior by stimulus satiation and food reinforcement. *Behavioral Research Therapy,* 1963, *1,* 53–61.

Ayllon, T., & Azrin, N. *The Token Economy: A Motivational System for Therapy and Rehabilitation.* New York: Appleton, 1968.

Back, K. W. The group can comfort but it can't cure. *Psychology Today,* 1972, 6, 28.

Baer, D. M. A case for selective reinforcement of punishment. In C. Neuringer and J. Michael (Eds.), *Behavior Modification in Clinical Psychology.* New York: Appleton, 1970.

Baer, D. M. Let's take another look at punishment. *Psychology Today,* 1971, 5, 32.

Bakan, D. The mystery-mastery complex in contemporary psychology. *American Psychologist,* 1965, 20, 186–191.

Bakan, D. *On Method: Toward a Reconstruction of Psychological Investigation.* San Francisco: Jossey-Bass, 1967.

Bakan, D. *Slaughter of the Innocents.* San Francisco: Jossey-Bass, 1971.

Bakan, D. Psychology can now kick the science habit. *Psychology Today,* 1972, 5, 26.

Bales, R. F. *Interaction Process Analysis: A Method for the Study of Small Groups.* Reading, Mass.: Addison-Wesley, 1950.

Barker, R. G. *Ecological Psychology.* Stanford: Stanford University Press, 1968.

Barker, R. G. Wanted: An eco-behavioral science. In Edwin P. Willems and Harold L. Raush (Eds.), *Naturalistic Viewpoints in Psychological Research.* New York: Holt, Rinehart and Winston, 1969. Pp. 31–43.

Beck, A. T. Reliability of psychiatric diagnosis: A critique of systematic studies. *American Journal of Psychiatry,* 1962, 119, 210–216.

Becker, H. *Outsiders.* New York: Free Press, 1963.

Bellak, L. *Schizophrenia: A Review of the Syndrome.* New York: Logos Press, 1958.

Bergmann, G., & Spence, K. W. The logic of psychophysical measurement. *Psychological Review,* 1944, 51, 1–24.

Bettelheim, B. The roots of radicalism. *Playboy,* March 1971.

Blissett, M. *Politics in Science.* Boston: Little, Brown, 1972.

Blixt, Sonya, & Ley, R. Effects of differential force-contingent reinforcement schedules on the frustration effect: A test of alternation hypotheses. *Proceedings of 76th Annual Convention of the American Psychological Association,* 1968. Pp. 127–128.

Braginsky, D. D. Machiavellianism and manipulative interpersonal behavior in children. *Journal of Experimental Social Psychology,* 1970, 6 (1), 77–97.

Braginsky, B. M., Braginsky, D. D., & Edwards, M. The political attitudes of mental patients and their "keepers." (In preparation.)

Braginsky, B. M., Braginsky, D. D., & Ring, K. *Methods of Madness: The Mental Hospital as a Last Resort.* New York: Holt, Rinehart and Winston, 1969.

Braginsky, D. D., & Braginsky, B. M. *Hansels and Gretels: Studies of Children in Institutions for the Mentally Retarded.* New York: Holt, Rinehart and Winston, 1971.

Braginsky, D. D., Braginsky, B. M., & Fitzgerald, J. The politics of psychodiagnosis. (In preparation.)

Brayfield, A. Report of the executive officer: 1966. *American Psychologist,* 1966, *21,* 1121.

Breland, Keller, & Breland, Marian. The misbehavior of organisms. *American Psychologist,* 1961, *16,* 681–684.

Bucher, B., & Lovaas, O. I. Use of aversive stimulation in behavior modification. In M. R. Jones (Ed.), *Miami Symposium on the Prediction of Behavior, 1967: Aversive Stimulation.* Miami: University of Miami Press, 1968.

Bugental, J. F. T. Humanistic psychology: a new break-through. *American Psychologist,* 1963, *18,* 563–567.

Bugental, J. F. T. The humanistic ethic—the individual in psychotherapy as a societal change agent. *Journal of Humanistic Psychology,* 1971, *10,* 11–25.

Cautela, J. R. Tie line (dirty sex). *Psychology Today,* 1971, *5,* 10.

Chapman, L. J., & Chapman, J. Genesis of popular but erroneous psychodiagnostic observations. *Journal of Abnormal Psychology,* 1967, *72,* 193–204.

Chapman, L. J., & Chapman, J. Illusory correlation as an obstacle to the use of valid psycho-diagnostic signs. *Journal of Abnormal Psychology,* 1969, *74,* 271–280.

Chapman, L. J., & Chapman, J. Test results are what you think they are. *Psychology Today,* 1971, *5,* 18.

Chein, I. *The Science of Behavior and the Image of Man.* New York: Basic Books, 1972.

Christie, R., Friedman, L. N., & Ross, A. The new left and its ideology. *Proceedings of 77th Annual Convention of the American Psychological Association,* 1969, 229–230.

Criswell, E. & Peterson, S. The whole soul catalog. *Psychology Today,* 1972, *5,* 57–64.

Delay, J., Pichot, P., & Perse, J. La notion de debilite mentale camouflee. *Annals of Medical Psychology,* 1952, *110,* 615–619.

Deutsch, A. *The Mentally Ill in America.* (2d ed.) New York: Columbia University Press, 1949.

Efron, C. Psychiatric bias: An experimental study of the effects of social class membership on diagnostic outcome. Unpublished master's thesis, Wesleyan University, 1970.

Ellis, A. Rational psychotherapy. In H. J. Eysenck (Ed.), *Experiments in Behaviour Therapy.* Oxford, England: Pergamon Press, 1967. Pp. 287–324.

Erikson, K. T. Notes on the sociology of deviance. *Social Problems.* (Spring) 1962, *9,* 308.

Evans, R. I. *B. F. Skinner—The Man and His Idea.* New York: E. P. Dutton, 1968.

Eysenck, H. J. *The Effects of Psychotherapy.* New York: International Science Press, 1966.

Farber, B. *Mental Retardation: Its Social Context and Social Consequences.* Boston: Houghton Mifflin, 1968.

Fernald, N. E. The burden of feeblemindedness. *Journal of Psychoasthenics,* 1912, *17,* 87–111.

Ferster, C. B., & Perrott, M. C. *Behavior Principles.* New York: Appleton, 1968.

Festinger, L., & Katz, D. *Research Methods in the Behavioral Sciences.* New York: Holt, Rinehart and Winston, 1953.

Festinger, L., Riecken, H. W., & Schachter, S. *When Prophecy Fails: A Social and Psychological Study of a Modern Group that Predicted the Destruction of the World.* Minnesota: University of Minnesota Press, 1956.

Foucault, M. *Madness and Civilization.* New York: Random House, 1965*a.*

Foucault, M. *Madness and Civilization: A History of Insanity in the Age of Reason.* New York: Pantheon Books, 1965*b.*

Freud, S. Postscript to a discussion on lay analysis (1927). In E. Jones (Ed.), *The Collected Papers of Sigmund Freud.* London: Hogarth, 1956.

Friedrichs, R. W. Mirror, mirror on the wall, what's the freest science of all? *Psychology Today,* 1971, *5,* 30.

Garfinkel, H. Conditions of successful degradation ceremonies. *American Journal of Sociology,* 1956, *61,* 420–424.

Giorgi, A. *Psychology as a Human Science.* New York: Harper & Row, 1970.

Glenn, M. On training therapists. In J. Agel (Prod.), *The Radical Therapist,* New York: Ballantine, 1971.

Gouldner, A. W. Anti-Minotaur: The myth of a value-free sociology. *Social Problems,* 1962, *9,* 199–213.

Gouldner, A. W. *The Coming Crisis of Western Sociology*. New York: Basic Books, 1970.

Graziano, A. M. In the mental-health industry, illness is our most important product. *Psychology Today*, 1972, 5, 12.

Greenberg, D. S. *The Politics of Pure Science*. New York: The New American Library, 1967.

Greenstein, F. *Personality and Politics*. Chicago: Markham, 1969.

Guthrie, E. R. *The Psychology of Learning*. New York: Harper & Row, 1935.

Haberer, J. Politicalization in science. *Science*, 1972, *178*, 713–723.

Haigh, G. V. Letter to the Editor. *Psychology Today*, 1969, 3, 4.

Haley, J. *The Power Tactics of Jesus Christ and Other Essays*. New York: Grossman Publishers, 1969.

Harre, R. Foreword. In S. M. Lyman & M. B. Scott (Eds.), *A Sociology of the Absurd*. New York: Appleton, 1970.

Harris, T. G. All the world's a box. *Psychology Today*, 1971, 5, 33–35.

Hartshorne, H., & May, M. A. *Studies in Deceit*. General Method and Results, Book 1; Statistical Methods and Results, Book 2. New York: Macmillan, 1928.

Heber, R. F. A manual on terminology and classification in mental retardation. *American Journal of Mental Deficiency*, Monograph Supplement, 1959, *64*, No. 2.

Heber, R. F. Mental retardation: concepts and classification. In E. Trapp & P. Hunelstein (Eds.), *Readings on the Exceptional Child*. New York: Appleton, 1962.

Helfand, I. Role taking in schizophrenia. *Journal of Consulting Psychology*, 1956, *20*, 37–41.

Hilgard, E. R. *Introduction to Psychology*. New York: Harcourt, 1962.

Hoffer, E. *The True Believer*. New York: Harper & Row, 1951.

Hollingshead, A. B., & Redlich, F. C. *Social Class and Mental Illness: A Community Study*. New York: Wiley, 1958.

Homans, G. C. *The Nature of Social Science*. New York: Harcourt, 1967.

Hull, C. L. *Principles of Behavior*. New York: Appleton, 1943.

Joint Commission on Mental Illness and Health. *Action for Mental Health*. New York: Basic Books, 1961.

Jordan, N. *Themes in Speculative Psychology*. London: Tavistock Publications Ltd., 1968.

Kanner, L. Feeblemindedness: Absolute, relative and apparent. *The Nervous Child*, 1948, 7, 365–397.

Kassorla, I. For catatonia: smiles, praise and a food basket. *Psychology Today,* 1969, *3,* 39–41.

Keen, S. Sing the body electric. *Psychology Today,* 1970, *4,* 56.

Kelman, H. C. *A Time To Speak: On Human Values and Social Research.* San Francisco: Jossey-Bass, 1968.

Kitsuse, J. I. Societal reactions to deviant behavior: Problems of theory and method. *Social Problems,* Winter 1962, *9,* 348.

Koch, E. Epilogue. Some trends of study I. In S. Koch (Ed.), *Psychology: A Study of a Science.* Vol. 3. New York: McGraw-Hill, 1935.

Koch, E. Psychological science versus the science-humanism antimony: Intimations of a significant science of man. *American Psychologist,* 1961, *16,* 629–639.

Koch, S. Psychology and emerging conceptions of knowledge as unitary. In T. W. Wann (Ed.), *Behaviorism and Phenomenology.* Chicago: University of Chicago Press, 1964.

Koch, S. Psychology cannot be a coherent science. *Psychology Today,* 1969, *3,* 14.

Koch, S. The image of man implicit in encounter group theory. *Journal of Humanistic Psychology,* 1971, *11,* 109–128.

Koestler, A. *Ghost in the Machine.* New York: Macmillan, 1968.

Kohlberg, L. Development of moral character and ideology. In M. L. Hoffman (Ed.), *Review of Child Development Research.* Russell Sage, 1964.

Köhler, W. *Gestalt Psychology: An Introduction to New Concepts in Modern Psychology.* New York: Liveright, 1947.

Krech, D. Does behavior really need a brain? In praise of William James: Some historical musings, vain lamentations and a sounding of great expectation. In R. B. McLeod (Ed.), *William James: Unfinished Business.* Washington, D.C.: American Psychological Association, 1969.

Kreitman, N. The reliability of psychiatric diagnosis. *Journal of Mental Science,* 1961, *107,* 876–886.

Kuhn, T. S. *The Structure of Scientific Revolution.* Chicago: University of Chicago Press, 1962.

Kupers, T. Radical therapy needs revolutionary theory. In J. Agel (Prod.), *The Radical Therapist.* New York: Ballantine, 1971.

Kushner, M. Faradic aversive controls in clinical practice. In C. Neuringer & J. L. Michael (Eds.), *Behavior Modification in Clinical Psychology.* New York: Appleton, 1970.

Laing, R. *The Politics of Experience.* New York: Pantheon, 1967.

Larrabee, E. Science and the common reader. *Commentary,* June 1966.

Latane, B., & Darley, J. M. Group inhibition of bystander intervention in emergencies. *Journal of Personality and Social Psychology,* 1968, *10,* 215–221.

Latane, B., & Darley, J. M. Bystander apathy. *American Scientist,* 1969, *57,* 244–268.

Lee, S. Social class bias in the diagnosis of mental illness. Ann Arbor, Michigan: University Microfilms, 1968.

Leifer, R. *In the Name of Mental Health: The Social Functions of Psychiatry.* New York: Science House, 1969.

Lewin, K. *A Dynamic Theory of Personality.* New York: McGraw-Hill, 1965.

Lewin, K. *Principles of Topological Psychology.* New York: McGraw-Hill, 1936.

Lewin, K. Formalization and progress in psychology. *University of Iowa Studies in Child Welfare,* 1940, *16*(3).

Little, K. B. Bazelon challenge requires soul searching. *American Psychological Association Monitor,* 1972, *3,* 2.

London, P. *The Modes and Morals of Psychotherapy.* New York: Holt, Rinehart and Winston, 1964.

McConnell, J. W. Criminals can be brainwashed—now. *Psychology Today,* 1970, *3,* 14.

McGinnis, J. *The Selling of the President 1968.* New York: Pocket Books, 1969.

Machiavelli, N. *The Prince and the Discourses.* New York: Modern Library, 1950.

MacLeod, R. B. The teaching of psychology and the psychology we teach. *American Psychologist,* 1965, *20,* 344–352.

Margolis, J. Freedom as determinism. *Society,* September/October 1972, *9,* 80–90.

Marrow, A. J. *The Practical Theorist: The Life and Work of Kurt Lewin.* New York: Basic Books, 1969.

Maslow, A. H. Eupsychia, the good society. *Journal of Humanistic Psychology,* 1961, *1,* 1–11.

Maslow, A. H. A theory of metamotivation: the biological rooting of the value-life. *Journal of Humanistic Psychology,* 1967, *7,* 93–127.

Matza, D. *Becoming Deviant.* New York: Prentice-Hall, 1969.

May, R. *Newsletter of Association for Humanistic Psychology.* January 1972.

Medvedev, Z. A., & Medvedev, R. A. *A Question of Madness.* New York: Knopf, 1971.

Merton, R. K. *Social Theory and Social Structure* (2d ed.) New York: Free Press, 1967.

Miller, N. E. Learnable drives and rewards. In S. S. Stevens (Ed.), *Handbook of Experimental Psychology*. New York: Wiley, 1951.

Miller, S. M., Riessman, F., & Seagull, A. A. Poverty and self-indulgence: a critique of the non-deferred pattern. In L. A. Farman, J. L. Kornbluh, & A. Haber (Eds.), *Poverty in America*. Ann Arbor: University of Michigan Press, 1968.

Moriarty, J. Psychologists protest testing of black children in California. *American Psychological Association Monitor*, 1972, 3 (3), 4.

Mowrer, O. H. *Learning Theory of Personality Dynamics*. New York: Ronald Press, 1950.

Moynihan, D. P. Eliteland. *Psychology Today*, 1970, *4*, 35.

Myrdal, G. *Objectivity in Social Research*. New York: Pantheon Books, 1969.

NISP Technical Report No. 15. Some preliminary results from a survey of graduate students in psychology. American Psychological Association, 1970.

Orne, M. T. On the social psychology of the psychological experiment: with particular emphasis to demand characteristics and their implications. *American Psychologist*, 1962, *17*, 776–783.

Pervin, L. A. Existentialism, psychology, and psychotherapy. *American Psychologist*, 1960, *15*, 305–309.

Polanyi, M. *Personal Knowledge*. Chicago: University of Chicago Press, 1958.

President's Panel on Mental Retardation. *A Proposed Program for National Action to Combat Mental Retardation*. Washington, D.C.: GPO, 1962.

Redlich, F. & Freedman, D. *The Theory and Practice of Psychiatry*. New York: Basic Books, 1966.

Rice, B. Skinner: the most important influence in psychology? *New York Times Magazine*, March 17, 1968.

Richman, B. F., Kellner, H. N., & Allen, D. Size constancy in retarded versus normal children: a developmental hypothesis. *Journal of Consulting and Clinical Psychology*, 1968, *32*, 579–582.

Ring, K. Experimental social psychology: Some sober questions about some frivolous values. *Journal of Experimental Social Psychology*, 1967, *3*, 113–123.

Rogers, C. The group comes of age. *Psychology Today*, 1969, *3*, 27.

Rosenhan, D. L. On being sane in insane places. *Science*, 1973, *179*, 250–257.

Rosenthal, R. *Experimenter Effects in Behavioral Research*. New York: Appleton, 1966.

Rotenberg, M. The protestant ethic and the "anti-labeling crusade": A critical reformulation. Unpublished manuscript, 1972.

Sanford, N. Will psychologists study human problems? *American Psychologist,* 1965, *20,* 192–202.

Sarason, S. B., & Doris, J. *Psychological Problems in Mental Deficiency.* (4th ed.) New York: Harper & Row, 1969.

Sarbin, T. On the futility of the proposition that some people be labeled "mentally ill." *Journal of Consulting Psychology,* 1967, *31,* 447–453.

Schaefer, H. H., & Martin, P. L. *Behavioral Therapy.* New York: McGraw-Hill, 1969.

Scheff, T. J. *Being Mentally Ill: A Sociological Theory.* Chicago: Aldine, 1966.

Schmitt, H. O., & Fonda, C. P. The reliability of psychiatric diagnosis: A new look. *Journal of Abnormal and Social Psychology,* 1956, *52,* 262–267.

Schooler, C., & Parkel, D. The overt behavior of chronic schizophrenics and its relationship to their internal state and personal history. *Psychiatry,* 1966, *29,* 67–77.

Schur, E. M. *Labeling Deviant Behavior.* New York: Harper & Row, 1971.

Sherwood, J. J., & Nataupsky, M. Predicting the conclusions of negro-white intelligence research from biographical characteristics of the investigator. *Journal of Personality and Social Psychology,* 1968, *8,* 53–58.

Shostrom, E. L. Group therapy: Let the buyer beware. *Psychology Today,* 1969, *2,* 37–40.

Sjoberg, G., & Nett, R. *A Methodology for Social Research.* New York: Harper & Row, 1968.

Skinner, B. F. *The Behavior of Organisms: An Experimental Analysis.* New York: Appleton, 1938.

Skinner, B. F. *Science and Human Behavior.* New York: Macmillan, 1953.

Skinner, B. F. *Beyond Freedom and Dignity.* New York: Knopf, 1971.

Smith, M. B. *Social Psychology and Human Values.* Chicago: Aldine, 1969.

Sonneman, U. *Existence and Therapy.* New York: Grune & Stratton, 1954.

Sorokin, P. *Fads and Foibles in Modern Sociology.* Chicago: Regnery, 1956.

Spence, K. W. *Behavior Theory and Conditioning.* New Haven: Yale University Press, 1956.

Steiner, C. Radical psychiatry and movement groups. In J. Agel (Prod.), *The Radical Therapist,* New York: Ballantine, 1971.

Szasz, T. *The Myth of Mental Illness.* New York: Hoeber, 1961.

Szasz, T.: *Law, Liberty and Psychiatry: An Inquiry into the Social Uses of Mental Health Practices.* New York: Crowell-Collier and Macmillan, 1963.

Szasz, T. *The Manufacture of Madness.* New York: Harper & Row, 1970.

Time. Skinner's Utopia: Panacea, or Path to Hell? Sept. 20, 1971.

Watson, J. B. Psychology as the behaviorist views it. *Psychological Review,* 1913, *20,* 158–177.

Weintraub, W., & Aronson, H. Social background of the patient in classical psychoanalysis. *Journal of Nervous and Mental Disease,* 1968, *146,* 91–97.

Wenger, D. L., & Fletcher, C. R. The effect of legal counsel on admission to a state mental hospital: A confrontation of professions. *Journal of Health and Social Behavior,* 1969, *10*(1), 66–72.

White, W. F. Pigeons, persons and piece rates. *Psychology Today,* 1972, *5,* 67–69.

Wolfle, D. Preface. In Koch, S. (Ed.), *Psychology: A Study of a Science.* Vol. 3. New York: McGraw-Hill, 1959.

Yospe, L. P. Ruminations—philosophical and otherwise. Unpublished manuscript, 1972.

Zigler, E., & Phillips, L. Psychiatric diagnosis and symptomatology. *Journal of Abnormal and Social Psychology,* 1961, *63,* 69–75.

Zilboorg, G., & Henry, G. *A History of Medical Psychology.* New York: Norton, 1941.

Ziman, John. *Public Knowledge: The Social Dimension of Science.* Cambridge: Cambridge University Press, 1968.

Index

A

Action therapy, 137–138
Adler, Alfred, 187
Adorno, T. W., 106, 189
Agel, J., 162, 189
Allen, D., 96, 196
Allport, G. W., 2, 76, 189
Altered States of Consciousness Induction Device (ASCID), 83
American Psychiatric Association, 189
American Psychoanalytic Association, 139
American Psychological Association, 32, 34, 63, 85, 86, 135
Anderson, Barry F., 12, 13, 14, 189

Aptitude tests, 117, 166
Aronson, H., 136, 198
Asch, S. E., 61, 83, 172–173, 184, 189
Ash, P., 119, 127, 189
Association for Humanistic Psychology, 76, 80, 84, 86
Authoritarian Personality, The (Adorno, Frenkel-Brunswik, Levinson, & Sanford), 106
Ayllon, T., 66, 71, 144–145, 147, 189, 190
Azrin, N., 66, 71, 144–145, 190

B

Back, K. W., 190
Bacon, Francis, 31

Baer, D. M., 151–153, 154, 157–
    158, 190
Bakan, D., 2, 16, 18, 28, 53, 83,
    91, 103, 190
Bales, R. F., 175, 190
Barker, R. G., 2, 173–174, 175,
    190
Bazelon, David L., 38
Beck, A. T., 119, 160, 190
Becker, H., 112, 190
Behavior, modification of, 43–73
    relationship between depriva-
        tion and, 141
    therapy and biting, 149–150
    See also Psychotherapy
Behaviorism, 43–73, 75, 76, 86,
        140–141, 147, 154–158,
        171, 172
    jargon and, 58–62
    methodolatry of, 46–58
    See also Psychotherapy
Being-values, 76
Bellak, L., 190
Bergmann, G., 22–23, 38, 190
Bettelheim, B., 190
Bias, 19, 20, 33, 62, 118, 120,
        121, 122
Bindrim, Paul, 85
Binet, Alfred, 114
Biting behavior, therapy and,
        149–150
Blissett, M., 5, 31, 190
Blixt, Sonya, 48–49, 50, 190
Braginsky, B. M., 115, 121, 122,
        123, 128, 132, 175, 191
Braginsky, D. D., 106, 115, 121,
        122, 123, 128, 132, 175,
        190, 191
Brayfield, A., 135, 191
Breland, Keller, 70–71, 191
Breland, Marian, 70–71, 191
Buber, Martin, 77
Bucher, B., 157, 191
Bugental, J. F. T., 2, 77, 82, 83,
        91, 159, 191

C

California State Department of
    Education, 118, 167
Calvin, John, 27
Cautela, J. R., 150–151, 191
Chapman, J., 118, 191
Chapman, L. J., 118, 191
Chein, I., 4, 178, 191
Child-abuse, study of, 103
Christie, R., 122, 191
Client-centered therapy, 136
Clinical psychology, 171
Comte, Auguste, 6
Conditioning, operant, 70, 142–
    143, 145
Control, 19–20
    prediction and, 15–17, 45
Covert sensitization technique,
    150–151
Criswell, E., 77, 83, 191
"Crotch-eyeballing" technique,
    85
Cruelty, study of, 103
    therapy and, 151

D

Daily activities, psychology and,
    36–39
Darley, J. M., 175, 195
Darwin, Charles, 25
Deceit in children, study of,
    105–106
Deferred Gratification Pattern,
    116
Delay, J., 119, 191
Deprivation, relationship be-
    tween behavior and, 141
Descartes, René, 25
Deutsch, A., 192
Deviants, 112–132, 167
    psychodiagnosing of, 117–120
    psychotherapy and, 133–164

Diagnosis, 111–132, 133
   of "diagnosis," 120–126
   of diagnostic labels, 126–129
   differential, 121
   relationship between social
      class and outcome of,
      120–121
   as stereotype, 129–132
Diagnostic labels, 133–134
   examination of, 126–129
Diagnostic testing, 117
Differential diagnosis, 121
Doris, J., 117, 197
Draw-a-Person test, 118

E

Edwards, M., 122, 191
Efron, C., 120, 131, 192
Electric shock, 148–150
Ellis, A., 163, 192
Elmer, Elizabeth, 103
Empirical observation, principle
   of, 12–13
Encounter groups (see Human-
      istic psychology)
Erikson, K. T., 112, 129, 192
Evans, R. I., 156, 192
Existentialism, 75
Eperimental psychology, 171
Extinction, Law of, 66, 72, 141
Extractive techniques, 55–56
Eysenck, H. J., 192

F

Faradic aversive controls, 148,
   171
Farber, B., 130, 192
Feeblemindedness, 114–115, 128
Fernald, N. E., 114–115, 192
Ferster, C. B., 59, 192
Festinger, L., 47, 53, 174, 192

Fetishism, therapy and, 149
Fitzgerald, J., 123, 191
Fletcher, C. R., 125–126, 198
Fonda, C. P., 119, 197
Foucault, M., 30, 111, 192
Frank, Jerome, 134
Freedman, D., 115, 196
Frenkel-Brunswik, E., 106, 189
Freud, S., 29, 89, 136, 163, 168,
   192
Friedman, L. N., 191
Friedrichs, R. W., 34, 192
Fromm, Erich, 76

G

Garfinkel, H., 132, 192
Giorgi, A., 2, 22, 192
Glenn, M., 162, 192
Goebbels, Paul Joseph, 156
Goldstein, Kurt, 76
Goldwater, Barry, 9, 98–99, 122
Gouldner, A. W., 6, 27, 35, 36,
   37, 192, 193
Graziano, A. M., 134, 193
Greenberg, D. S., 8, 9, 11, 31,
   32, 193
Greenstein, F., 99, 100, 193
Guthrie, E. R., 66, 193

H

Haberer, J., 31, 193
Haigh, G. V., 80–81, 193
Haley, J., 113, 127, 193
Harre, R., 19, 193
Harris, T. G., 30, 193
Hartshorne, H., 105, 193
Hebb, D. O., 168
Heber, R. F., 115, 127, 128, 193
Helfand, I., 95–96, 193
Helmholtz, Hermann, 25
Henry, G., 198

Hilgard, E. R., 26, 193
Hitler, Adolf, 72, 156
Hobbes, Thomas, 11
Hoffer, E., 169, 193
Hollingshead, A. B., 120, 131, 193
Homans, G. C., 175–176, 193
Homosexuality, therapy and, 150–151
Horney, Karen, 76
Hull, C. L., 56–58, 61, 66, 89, 137, 193
Humanistic Ethic, 77
Humanistic psychology, 43, 44, 75–87, 171
  jargon and, 77–83
  technolatry and, 83
Humanistic psychotherapy, 159–161
Hume, David, 25
Hypotheses, 18–20, 48–50, 55

I

Imagery technique, 150–151
Industrial psychology, 171
Insight therapy, 136–137, 138, 163
Intelligence, Jensen theory of, 34
  measurement of, 114, 117, 118–119, 166, 167
Introspection, 172

J

James, William, 3, 104–105, 131, 187
Jargon (see Language)
Jensen theory of intelligence, 34
Job satisfaction, 145
Johnson, Lyndon B., 41

Joint Commission on Mental Illness and Health, 193
Jordan, N., 2–3, 105, 193
Journal of Humanistic Psychology, 75

K

Kanner, L., 128, 193
Kassorla, I., 141–143, 194
Katz, D., 192
Keen, S., 160–161, 194
Kellner, H. N., 96, 196
Kelman, H. C., 94, 194
Kitsuse, J. I., 112, 194
Koch, E., 194
Koch, S., 2, 4, 10, 22, 26–27, 44, 46, 80, 81, 84–85, 86, 91, 161, 194
Koestler, A., 72, 73, 194
Kohlberg, L., 194
Köhler, W., 167, 172, 194
Krech, D., 3, 194
Kreitman, N., 119, 127, 194
Krieck, Ernst, 31
Kuhn, T. S., 22, 194
Kupers, T., 163, 194
Kushner, M., 148–150, 194

L

Labeling, purpose of, 132
Labels, diagnostic, 133–134
  examination of, 126–129
Laing, R., 113, 127, 194
Landon, Alfred, 15
Language, humanistic psychology and, 77–83
  methodolatry and, 62–63
  psychology and, 56–63
Larrabee, E., 25, 194
Latané, B., 175, 195
Lear, Edward, 63

Learning, 177–186
Lee, S., 120, 131, 195
Leifer, R., 113, 127, 134, 136–137, 138, 139, 157, 195
Levinson, D. J., 106, 189
Lewin, K., 168, 176, 187, 195
Ley, R., 48–49, 50, 190
Life space, 176–177, 182
Little, K. B., 38–39, 195
Locke, John, 25
London, P., 134, 136, 137, 139, 155, 164, 195
Lovaas, O. I., 157, 191

M

McConnell, J. W., 153, 156, 157, 195
McGinnis, J., 72, 195
Machiavelli, N., 152, 195
MacLeod, R. B., 2, 3, 4, 10, 29, 195
Margolis, J., 46, 195
Marrow, A. J., 176, 195
Martin, P. L., 141, 146, 154, 197
Marxism, oppression by, 163
Maslow, A. H., 30, 75–82, 84, 85, 89, 170, 195
Matza, D., 114, 132, 195
May, M. A., 105, 193
May, R., 86, 195
Mediator, scientist as, 7
Medici, 156
Medvedev, R. A., 33, 122, 195
Medvedev, Z. A., 33, 122, 195
Mental retardation, definitions of, 128
Merton, R. K., 27–28, 30, 31, 195
Metamotivation, Theory of, 76, 78, 81
Methodolatry, 29, 46
    behaviorism and, 46–58
    jargon and, 62–63

Miller, N. E., 66, 168, 195
Miller, S. M., 116, 196
Mills, C. W., 6
Misfits (see Deviants)
Moralizer, scientist as, 5–6
Moriarty, J., 119, 196
Movements, 169
Mowrer, O. H., 66, 196
Moynihan, D. P., 196
Myrdal, G., 22, 26, 27, 28, 32, 38, 39, 44, 62, 73, 77, 90, 102, 103, 196

N

Nataupsky, M., 34, 197
National Academy of Sciences, 31–32
Nazis, 156
Nett, R., 5, 6, 22, 197
Nixon, Richard M., 72

O

Operant conditioning, 70, 142–143, 145
Operational definition, principle of, 13–14
Orne, M. T., 19, 23, 53, 55, 196

P

Parkel, D., 115, 197
Participant-observer, technique, 175
Pavlov, I., 137
Pearson, Karl, 25
Perls, Fritz, 161
Perrott, M. G., 59, 192
Perse, J., 119, 191
Personality tests, 117, 166
Pervin, L. A., 2, 196

Peter the Great, 33
Peterson, S., 77, 83, 191
Phillips, L., 119
Piaget, Jean, 168
Pichot, P., 119, 191
Pierce, William, 119
Polanyi, M., 22, 196
Politics, psychology and, 30–36,
     98–100, 122–125
Poor, studies of the, 116–117
Prediction and control, princi-
     ple of, 15–17, 45
Predestination, doctrine of, 113
President's Panel on Mental Re-
     tardation, 121, 128, 196
Prognosis, social class and, 120–
     121
Protestant Ethic, 113, 116
Psychoanalysis, 136, 139
Psychodiagnosis, 117–132, 133
Psychodiagnostic tests, 117–120
Psychologists, activities of, 5
     as scientists, 5, 9–11
Psychology, clinical, 171
     criticisms of, 1–4, 37–38
     daily activities and, 36–39
     defining, 4–5, 39, 43, 44
     evaluation of, guidelines for,
        169–170
     experimental, 171
     future of, 165, 186
     history of, 25–28
     humanistic, 43, 44, 75–87, 171
        jargon and, 77–83
        technolatry and, 83
     industrial, 171
     language and, 56–63
     maiden functions of, 129–130
     mission of, 30
     politics and, 30–36, 98–100,
        122–125
     present-day, 1–24, 40, 86–87,
        186–187
     rack as paradigm for, 91–97
     religion and, 28–30, 76, 101

     social, 171–172
     sociology of, 25–41
     subject matter of, 4
     task of, 45
Psychotherapy, 133–164
     definition of, 139–140
     humanistic, 159–161
Punishment, as therapy, 147–
     154, 157–158
Purist, scientist as, 8–9

R

Rack, as paradigm for psychol-
     ogy, 91–97
Radical therapy, 162–163
Raimy, Victor, 139
Redlich, F. C., 115, 120, 131,
     193, 196
Reich, Wilhelm, 140
Reik, Theodore, 139
Reinforcement, 48–49, 66–68,
     71, 142–146, 184
     Law of, 66, 72, 141
Religion, psychology and, 28–
     30, 76, 101
Research, 89–109
     applied, 108–109
     design of, 17–24
     examples of, 46–57
Resocialization, 136
Retardates, studies of, 96–97,
     115
Retardation (see Mental retar-
     dation)
Rice, B., 70, 196
Richman, B. F., 96, 196
Riecken, H. W., 174, 192
Riessman, F., 116, 196
Ring, K., 121, 128, 171, 175,
     191, 196
Rogers, C., 76, 81, 82, 136, 168,
     196
Role-taking, study of, 95

Roosevelt, Franklin D., 15
Rorschach inkblot test, 118
Rosenhan, D. L., 131, 134, 175, 196
Rosenthal, R., 19, 23, 53, 196
Ross, A., 191
Rotenberg, M., 113, 196
Royal Society of London, 31

S

Salk, Jonas, 31
Sanford, N., 2, 91, 197
Sanford, R. N., 106, 189
Sarason, S. B., 117, 197
Sarbin, T., 30, 61, 114, 127, 197
Satiation, principle of, 147
Schachter, S., 174, 192
Schaefer, H. H., 141, 146, 154, 197
Scheff, T. J., 127, 197
Schizophrenia, 115, 120, 127, 142
Schmitt, H. O., 119, 197
Schooler, C., 115, 197
Schur, E. M., 197
Schutz, W., 89
Scientific enterprise, 11–12, 21, 93
    importance of language in, 56–57
Scientific method, 11, 16, 21, 46, 83, 90, 91
Scientists, psychologists as, 5, 9–11
    roles of, 5–9
    social, 5–9, 21
Seagull, A. A., 116, 196
Self-actualization, 75, 78, 79, 83
Sensitization (see Covert sensitization technique)
Serbsky Institute of Forensic Psychiatry, 33
Sherwood, J. J., 34, 197

Shock, electric, 148–150
Shostrom, E. L., 85, 197
Simon, Theodore, 114
Sjoberg, G., 5, 6, 22, 197
Skinner, B. F., 6, 20–21, 29, 30, 37, 44–45, 46, 58–59, 62–72, 78, 86, 89, 137, 145, 151, 155–156, 161, 168, 184, 197
Smith, M. B., 94, 197
Social class, prognosis and, 120–121
    relationship between diagnostic outcome and, 120–121
Social psychology, 171–172
Social scientists, 5–9, 21
Sociology of psychology, 25–41
Somatic therapy, 160–161
Sonneman, U., 2, 197
Sorokin, P., 197
Spence, K. W., 22–23, 38, 66, 190, 197
Stalin, Joseph, 156
Stampfl, T., 137
Statistical generalization, principle of, 14–15
Steiner, C., 162, 197
Stereotypes, diagnoses as, 129–132
Subjects, psychological, 54–55, 98–101, 107
Supreme Court, U.S., 41
Szasz, T., 92, 112, 113, 114, 127, 198

T

Technician, scientist as, 7–8
Technolatry, humanistic psychology and, 83
Testing, diagnostic, 117
Tests, aptitude, 117, 166
    Draw-a-Person, 118
    intelligence, 114, 117, 118–119, 166, 167

Tests, aptitude (*continued*)
  personality, 117, 166
  psychodiagnostic, 117–120
  Rorschach inkblot, 118
Therapeutic relationship, nature
  of, 137
Therapy, action, 137–138
  client-centered, 136
  insight, 136–137, 138, 163
  punishment as, 147–154, 157–
  158
  radical, 162–163
  somatic, 160–161
  See also Psychotherapy
"Third Force" movement (*see*
  Humanistic psychology)
Thorndike, Edward L., 137
"Token economy" motivational
  system, 144

                    U
Ullman, Walter, 112

                    V
Village Voice, 160

                    W

Watson, J. B., 44, 89, 198
Weber, Max, 35
Weintraub, W., 136, 198
Wenger, D. L., 125–126, 198
Werner, H., 96
White, W. F., 145, 198
Whole Soul Catalog (Criswell
  and Peterson), 83
Wofle, D., 2, 198
Wolpe, J., 137

                    Y

Yospe, L. P., 3, 22, 198

                    Z

Zigler, E., 119, 198
Zilboorg, G., 198
Ziman, John, 11, 13, 15–16, 17,
  198

Mainstream Psychology

is a systematic attack on the commonly held
assumptions about the nature of psychology and the
activities of psychologists. It is a painstaking analysis
of the schools of thought which constitute
psychology's mainstream and a revelatory inquiry
into the beliefs, attitudes, and motives of today's
practitioners.

The Braginskys, themselves professional
psychologists, write as much in hope as they do in
outrage over the failures and misdirections of the
discipline to which they have devoted their lives. In
stating why they undertook this critique of
psychology, they say:

"We are committed to the survival of psychology as a viable
system for truth-seeking. Our analysis and criticisms, then,
are borne out of concern that psychology is failing and has
become alienated from itself. So long as its foundations are
myths, absurdities, and pretensions, its demise is inevitable.
Our purpose for writing this book, therefore, was that it may
be used constructively in reshaping psychology."

They begin by exploding the myth about what
psychologists actually do.

"The standard definition of psychology would lead us to
believe that psychologists spend a good deal of their time
scientifically observing animal and human behavior. The
majority of the activities psychologists engage in, however,
do not fall within the realm of this definition. Psychologists
may lecture, grade papers, attend conferences, write
research reports, participate in committees, seek
promotions, conduct psychotherapy, or act as consultants.
That is, they are engaged in activities that maintain (and
usually increase) their economic and social status."